NEVER BE LATE AGAIN

Praise for
NEVER BE LATE AGAIN

"*Never Be Late Again* combines solid research with insightful solutions and humorous anecdotes. This intelligently written book will most certainly improve the lives and personal relationships of the punctually challenged."

—John Gray, Author
Men Are from Mars, Women Are from Venus

"Diana DeLonzor is doing a favor for the entire world with her very readable *Never Be Late Again*. It's fun to read, very instructive, and most of all, a blessing for timely people. I wish she had written it fifty years ago."

—Jay Conrad Levinson, Author
Guerrilla Marketing

"I can't think of anyone who wouldn't benefit from reading this book. I've recommended it to others both socially and professionally. It's not just in the office that punctuality matters."

—Bill Bednarski, Vice President of OEM and
Licensing Technology, Tyco International

Punctually Challenged
(punc´·tu·al·ly chal´·linjd) adj,
n, having the inexplicable
ability to arise at six, yet
still be late to work at nine

THE DOZEN BEST EXCUSES FOR BEING LATE

1. I'm trying to break this perfectionist image.
2. Wasn't it Einstein who first said time is relative?
3. Why do we need labels like "late"? Can't we all just get along?
4. I was busy planning a surprise party for you.
5. Really, I don't feel tardy.
6. My biorhythms are off.
7. Existentially speaking, how can you prove I'm late?
8. I'm protesting the oppressive nature of clocks.
9. Explain this whole "late" concept to me again.
10. I thought you might want some time alone.
11. I was born late, you know.
12. Mentally, I was here twenty minutes ago.

NEVER BE LATE AGAIN

7 Cures for the Punctually Challenged™

DIANA DELONZOR

POST MADISON PUBLISHING
SAN FRANCISCO, CALIFORNIA

Library of Congress Control Number 2002100633

ISBN 0-9716499-9-5

Other fine Post Madison Books are available from your local bookstore or directly from the publisher:

Post Madison Publishing
San Francisco, California 94123
info@postmadisonpublishing.com

10 9 8 7 6 5 4 3 2 1

PUBLISHER'S NOTE
The anecdotes described in this book are true. The individuals' names, as well as certain defining details and statements ascribed to such individuals, have been altered to protect the identities of the individuals on whom each anecdote is based.

CONTENTS

In memory of funny, beautiful Gwendy,
whose eyes I'm certain are looking down,
and whose laughter we all miss.

ACKNOWLEDGMENTS

I would like to express my deep gratitude to Larry Dan for his professional and personal assistance with this project. Heartfelt thanks go to my talented and patient photographers, Bernardo Grijalva and Todd Heapy, my creative cover designer, Irvin Lin and my production expert, John Eagle. Special appreciation also goes to my good friend Mary Ellen Warner, whose whose help and advice were invaluable.

I'm grateful as well to the many wonderful people who helped me along the way, including San Francisco State University psychology professors Jamie Newton and Dawn Terrell; Cleveland State University psychology professor Steve Slane; authors John Gray, Jay Levinson, David Lieberman, Ph.D, Neil Fiore, Ph.D., Stephan Bodian, Beckon, and Tracey Wood; Jane Massengill, MFCC; UPS publicity manager, Dan McMackin; editors Caroline Pincus and Margie Margeroux; readers Bill Heitner, Katherine Bretz, Louise and Bill Lidicker, Robert, Gerry, Russell, and Kim DeLonzor.

To view the web sites of my talented contributors, please visit:

Irvin Lin: www.jackhonky.com

Todd Heapy: www.thphoto.com

PART ONE

PUNCTUALLY CHALLENGED

Running Late

My most vivid memory of Laura and Robert's wedding is that I was late. It was a stiflingly hot summer day, and the ceremony was to take place at 5 p.m. on a country club golf course an hour's drive from my home in San Francisco. By the time I finally sped into the parking lot, hair flying and tires squealing, it was 5:10 (well OK, 5:20). Sprinting madly across the manicured lawns of the club, I headed toward a gathering of people seated in a roped-off area near the eighteenth hole.

The wedding hadn't yet started, so I wiped the sweat from my face, straightened my dress and began to tiptoe down the center aisle to find a seat. Just as I started though, the string quartet struck up Mendelssohn's "Wedding March." The guests all rose and turned to watch for the bride, but what they saw in the middle of the aisle was me. As the music swelled, I frantically looked for an empty spot amid the packed seats, but couldn't find a single chair. Suddenly I caught sight of the bride starting down the aisle a few yards behind me. She motioned for me to get out of the way, but with nowhere to sit and nowhere to hide, I could only smile, wave sheepishly, and try in vain to flatten myself against an aisle-side candelabra. As Laura drew nearer, I decided to make a break for it. Disentangling myself from the candelabra, I turned and dashed up the aisle toward the altar. Making a quick left in front of the surprised minister, I ran past the first row of guests, climbed over the velvet retaining rope and headed back toward the rear, where I remained, red faced, for the rest of the ceremony. Laura and Robert forgave me, but I still cringe with embarrassment when I relive that day.

—My own story

Have you ever suffered through an incident like this? If the answer is yes, you're not alone. An estimated 20 percent of the U.S. population have trouble getting to where they're going on time. The Punctually Challenged are everywhere. From homemakers to home builders, from CPAs to CEOs, we appear in all professions and join ranks with such reputedly late luminaries as former president Bill Clinton, supermodel Naomi Campbell, actors Robert Redford, Richard Gere and Rebecca Romijn and singers Cher and Mariah Carey.

Although some of the most talented and successful people in the world are devoted disciples of the adage "better late than never," many more of us have been passed over for promotions, forfeited raises and lost face with families and colleagues. While movie stars and politicians may wield enough power and influence to get away with living in the slow lane, for the rest of us, chronic tardiness can be a real liability. So if you've found yourself apologizing to irate dinner hostesses, pleading mercy from traffic cops, or inventing imaginative excuses once too often, this book is for you.

I am a former card-carrying member of the punctually challenged and punctuality used to be my Achilles heel. I was suspended three times in junior high school for tardiness. I've been late for surprise parties, client presentations, court appearances and classes for which I was the instructor. Planes, graduations and funerals have left, started and ended without me.

My belated arrival times embarrassed me and wreaked havoc in my personal and professional relationships. Friends and family members finally resorted to lying about the time an event began. If dinner was at 7:00, they told me 6:30. My assistant took to scheduling meetings at 9:15, knowing I couldn't reliably be counted on to show up any earlier. Evenings out on the town began with my husband calling, "I'm going down to start the car," knowing I'd feel terribly guilty if I continued to dawdle with him in the driveway and the motor running.

I hated being late and often resolved to improve my timeliness, but rarely with any success. One New Year's Day, I finally got serious about it. "I'll never be late again," I announced to my husband.

Eyeing me with disbelief, he replied, "I have an idea. Why don't you give yourself an extra fifteen minutes to get ready?" I thought about this remedy and realized it wasn't quite that simple—it was like suggesting a dieter simply stop eating so much. Besides, I could get up at 6:00 a.m. and still be late to work at 9:00. It began to dawn on me that I might be getting something out of my frantic rushing, from the whirlwinds I created for myself. Being on time meant figuring out what that something might be and learning to live without it.

After much research and introspection, I discovered that the excitement of having to rush gave me a jolt that motivated and spurred me on. I found that my need for stimulation was caused by a tendency to feel easily bored and restless. Once I saw why I liked to hurry—why I preferred the sprint to the stroll—not only did I leave the ranks of the punctually challenged, but I also began to procrastinate less in general. I started to plan my time more effectively and to use more organization in my daily affairs. As I worked toward the goal of being more timely, I began to see the importance of being a reliable person. Developing that side of myself soon became a priority.

But it wasn't easy. The truth is, chronic lateness can be a surprisingly difficult habit to overcome. Research indicates that in many ways, it's like overeating. Just as the dieter wakes in the morning resolved not to overindulge, the late person vows to be on time for work. Yet, just as the dieter falls victim to the chocolate-covered doughnut, the straggler succumbs to the temptation to do one last thing before leaving the house. Resisting that sudden urge to make the bed, unload the dishwasher, water the plants or finish a newspaper article can be nearly impossible.

While there are those who get a charge out of keeping others waiting—a condition I've found most prevalent among men (sorry guys)—if you're typical, you dislike being late. Chances are you've tried more than once to reform. Following each fiasco, you've sworn your late days are over. You'll turn over a new leaf, skip breakfast, get a new clock and stop shaving your legs in the morning. You've made all the right resolutions, yet tardiness remains your nemesis.

Biology or Psychology?

Psychologists have theories about late folks. Even Sigmund Freud had a hypothesis, believing lateness to be an anal characteristic. The child who had difficulty with toilet training, he hypothesized, would have a similarly challenging time when it came to other self-management tasks like punctuality.

Another look at the psychology of lateness comes from a 1991 Cleveland State University study in which trial participants underwent a number of psychological tests. Researchers found that the tardy subjects differed from their timely counterparts in a number of personality characteristics, with late people scoring measurably lower on nurturance and higher on both long- and short-term anxiety.

Do late people really differ from the timely in certain personality characteristics? I conducted a study in association with San Francisco State University aimed at asking that question and determining what causes chronic lateness. We studied 225 people who were given a battery of personality tests and questioned about their attitudes and habits relating to punctuality. As it turned out, the late scored higher in several areas, including anxiety and distractibility, while placing somewhat below the timely in the areas of self-esteem and self-discipline.

Could Late People Perceive Time Differently?

Part of my research included a test to measure the differences in how timely and late people perceive the passage of time. The test I devised is a simple one you can try yourself. Choose three or four pages in a book, mark the time and start reading. Stop when you think ninety seconds have elapsed, then check your watch to see how accurate you were. I found that early birds, almost without fail, stopped reading before ninety seconds had passed, while late people put their books down well after the ninety-second mark.

The researchers at Cleveland State University also included a time perception test in their study, this time using stopwatches. Interestingly, their results were similar to mine, with late people consistently underestimating the passage of time.

There are a number of theories for why these time-perception tests turned out the way they did. Although it's feasible that late people perceive time differently, it's likely there are other explanations as well. In later chapters, we'll take a closer look at the possible reasons behind the results.

It's Not Just Time Management

This is not merely a book about time management. Certainly, knowing how to be organized and efficient is key to being on time. The importance of establishing priorities, setting goals and proper planning cannot be overemphasized. However, consistent lateness is not caused by disorganization alone and time-management skills in themselves won't cure it.

Remember this important fact: Every time we perform an act, we get something out of it—a benefit. This is particularly true with negative habits. If there weren't some kind of payoff, we wouldn't continue them. Although we often suffer from our habits, we make decisions, consciously or not, based on the benefits versus the costs. One of the most important steps in changing any long-ingrained habit is figuring out what your particular benefit might be. Once you understand what's going on in your mind when you're late, you're halfway there.

Although your goal may be simple—to be more punctual—when you untangle the roots of the problem, you'll find yourself resolving other issues as well. You may be surprised to learn that the source of your lateness is something quite different than what you thought. It's much like peeling an onion—as you peel away the layers, you begin to see what's below.

Peeling the Onion

Susan, a reformed person said it well:

> *"I've always had a number of bad habits—procrastination and lateness among them—and I've struggled, usually without success, to overcome them. I realize now that I've been dealing with my habits on a superficial basis, never taking the time to really understand what was behind my behavior. Once I got on track, I began arriving at appointments and meetings early. Instead of the desperate dash to the finish line, I learned to walk in the door calmly. Now as I sit back and watch other people arriving late, flustered and apologetic, I have a quiet laugh to myself, reveling in the feeling of being so responsible and dependable.*
>
> *"When I finally discovered the keys to overcoming my tardiness, I solved much more than I thought I would. Changing this lifelong habit gave me more self-confidence and control over my life. I began to feel less like an anomaly, a butt of jokes. I imagine it's the way people feel when they finally lose weight."*

In the chapters to come, I'll discuss why punctuality is important, how you may have come to be punctually challenged, and what you can do to change. You'll find tips for overcoming lateness and exercises that correspond directly to your particular type of lateness.

The anecdotes contained in this book are based on the true stories of my clients and associates and are ones you'll undoubtedly relate to. While you'll likely associate most closely to one particular lateness type, please look through the exercises in each chapter. You'll find useful tools, such as tips for improving time perception and advice on overcoming procrastination, throughout the book. Although there are dozens of exercises, choose only three or four initially to start you on your way. When you've mastered those and are ready, select a few more.

Please be sure to review *A Few Words on Successful Habit Changing* near the end of the book. These summarize some fundamental habit-breaking concepts and will help you to stay focused on your goals.

Last but not least, I've included a chapter for the early birds in your life. Pass this along to your friends, family and associates, as it will help them better understand and support you as you work through the process of changing.

Changing any habit, much less an ongoing daily one, is not easy. Tom Rusk, M.D., author of *Instead of Therapy*, once said, "Resistance to change is the most powerful force in human psychology." Change takes time, effort, and the willingness to try something different. Bear in mind the old saying, "If you do what you've always done, you'll get what you've always gotten." It's really true. If the tactics you've used in the past haven't been effective by now, they probably won't be in the future. So commit to trying something new.

The habit of lateness is like any other habit. Even when you think you've finally broken the pattern, you'll find yourself backsliding. Be patient with yourself. You won't change overnight. But if you practice the techniques in this book on a daily basis, your days of rushing, apologizing and excuses will be over and you'll embrace a new, more effective way of managing your time and your life.

What's So Great About Being on Time?

A DeKalb County, GA juror who showed up for duty fifteen minutes late recently was thrown in jail.

—The Washington Times

The Best Laid Plans of Mice and Men…

Manila—In his effort to turn the Philippines from Asia's donkey into another regional tiger, President Fidel Ramos declared the week beginning April 12 to be "National Consciousness Week of the Imperative for Punctuality and Respect for the Rights of Others." Filipinos are reputed to have a relaxed and charming but sometimes infuriating Latin Mañana approach to life. President Ramos recognized that to be truly Asian and Confucian, you have to show you know that time is money and punctuality matters. So he decided to attend the launch of punctuality week himself. Unfortunately, he turned up an hour late. He had set his alarm for 4 a.m. in order to watch Tiger Woods's triumph in the U.S. Masters golf tournament, and after that exertion, overslept in the morning.

—St. Louis Dispatch

Is punctuality really so important? Or are early birds just too uptight? In the next few pages, you'll discover that there are, in fact, a number of excellent reasons for being punctual.

Perhaps you already have plenty of incentive to kick your tardiness habit and need no further convincing. If that's the case, please skip to the next chapter. If, however, you're not yet there, following are a few inducements to sway your thinking.

Great Reason #1: Tardiness Affects Your Self-Esteem

Most tardy people suffer from feelings of guilt and embarrassment. Although we struggle to rationalize—blaming the kids or the commute—deep down we know we're responsible. Chronic tardiness doesn't just sabotage our relationships with other people; it whittles away our own self-esteem. It can make us feel as though we are not in control of our lives.

Former punctually challenged folks, on the other hand, say that once they manage to change, they begin to build self-confidence, gain respect from other people and take more pride in themselves. They become more aware of why they perform certain habits, and feel less at the mercy of their compulsions. Here's what Andy, a reformed late person, had to say:

"I no longer get those disapproving looks, the ones I know mean, 'When is he going to get his act together?' It's a relief not to have to make up excuses for being late and my girlfriend is much happier with the new me."

Great Reason #2: It Impacts the Lives of Others

Tardiness is the biggest disrespect.

—Cindy Crawford

Why do the timely get so crabby over ten or fifteen minutes here or there? Is tardiness really worthy of such a fuss? Understand that a few minutes now and then really isn't important—if it happens once in a while. But when lateness is chronic, it can be downright annoying for those left waiting.

What's more, the timely take your lateness personally. They see tardiness as something you are doing to them. Perhaps they've cut short a workout at the gym, skipped breakfast or waved away a second cup of coffee. If they've made sacrifices to meet you on time, they'll feel frustrated and slighted that you didn't think enough of them to do the same. For the most part, prompt people believe that if you really wanted to, you'd show up on time.

Maybe you've been chastised severely only a handful of times, so you're not fully aware of the frustration you cause. "No one seems put out by my lateness," you conclude. "If they were really bothered, they would have said something." Unfortunately, many people simply swallow their frustration and never express what they're really thinking.

Great Reason #3: It makes a Bad Impression

In the course of researching this book, I interviewed many friends and family members of late people. The punctual voiced one opinion time and again—tardiness affects the degree of respect they have for you. In my group interviews with both types, the debates that broke out were ferocious. You could almost hear the perpetually prompt crying, "Off with their heads!" Here's just a sample of what they had to say:

"Late people believe their time is more important than yours."

"They like the attention they get when they walk into a room."

"It's a passive-aggressive thing. Late people want to be in control."

"They don't have the same respect for others."

While these sentiments may seem hurtful and are, for the most part untrue, it's important to understand the ways in which your lateness affects others' perceptions of you.

Great Reason #4: Lateness is a Career Buster

"When I showed up for work one day, my manager called me into his office to inform me I was being terminated for tardiness. Much to my surprise, as he spoke, he opened a small appointment book where he had noted every day I was late, going back two years."

—Mary Ellen, a former project manager

Tardiness costs American businesses more than $3 billion dollars each year in lost productivity and the business managers I interviewed ranked lateness as a primary employee-related problem. Ten minutes here and there adds up, they said. One executive pointed out that an employee who is ten minutes late to work every day has, in essence, taken a full week of unscheduled paid vacation time by the end of the year. And this lost productivity is only a small piece of the pie.

Managers overwhelmingly said they were less likely to promote persistently tardy employees because they're seen as people who lack discipline and enthusiasm. Chronically late employees not only affected the bottom line, they explained, but were also bad for morale in general. When an employee is repeatedly late, other employees wonder why they're knocking themselves out to get in on time.

Great Reason #5: In This Culture, Punctuality Matters

In many cultures, timeliness is not a priority. In some areas of Africa, the concept of time as we understand it doesn't even exist, and there are no equivalent words for "hour," "minute" or "second," no fixed definitions for early or late. It's day when the sun comes up, night when it sets. Synchronizing watches isn't terribly important—there are no planes to catch, no appointments to keep.

Even in some industrialized nations, time is viewed more as an estimate than an exact science. Brazilians, Spaniards, and Southeast Indians, for instance, don't value punctuality as highly as the Swiss, Germans or North Americans and have a pretty flexible idea of what's considered "on time." Guests to social events typically arrive an hour late, and hosts wouldn't dream of chastising a guest who kept them waiting.

Should we admire or disapprove of these laid-back societies? Certainly a clockless, relaxed way of life has its appeal—no trains or buses to run after, no excuses to make. But let's face it, in western cultures, the clock is part of our lives. It's a simple fact that in tightly scheduled societies, our timeliness (or lack thereof) affects other people and has a snowball effect.

Perhaps we're all too precise. But since it's unlikely we late folks will have much success convincing the majority of the industrialized world to loosen their standards, it may be a better use of our energies to join them and accept the fact that punctuality is important.

What Makes the Tardy So Tardy?

To tell persistently tardy people to "just do it" is like saying to a clinically depressed person, "just cheer up."

—Psychologist Joseph Ferrari

New York—He has been in office barely six months, but is already referred to as the late President Clinton—chronically late, that is. Often behind schedule, the nation's Chief Executive operates on what Washington jokingly—if at times ruefully—call Clinton Standard Time. Few have been spared Mr. Bill's waiting game. In January, Supreme Court Justice William Rehnquist cut short a meeting with Clinton after the President left him waiting for 45 minutes. On the morning of Inauguration Day, George and Barbara Bush were kept waiting at the White House for coffee with the Clintons. And at the Japan summit earlier this month, Clinton arrived 22 minutes late for a speech at Waseda University. Vice President Al Gore recently referred to the administration as "punctually challenged," and even wife Hillary conceded, "It's maddening to try to keep him on any kind of schedule."

—People Magazine

Have you ever wondered what causes a life-long tendency to run late? In previous chapters, we looked at some scientific theories about punctuality as well as some not so scientific—and rather stinging—comments put forth by early birds. In this chapter we'll take a closer look at common myths and truths and sort out which hold water.

Perception #1: Looking for Attention

A common perception among the timely is that late folks enjoy the attention they receive when they're the last ones to enter a room. Are we shameless spotlight stealers? In more than 300 interviews and 225 anonymous questionnaires, rarely did I come across anyone who enjoyed the recognition they got from their belated arrivals. Quite the opposite, actually. They dreaded being the last person to walk into a meeting, the final straggler to arrive at dinner. In fact, most envied timely folks because they seem so, well…together. As the tardy rush breathlessly into the room, they can't help but notice the early birds sitting calmly, sipping coffee, reviewing their notes or helping the hostess.

Of course, there are a number of attention seekers out there, but people like Lauren are more typical. "I'd rather not show up at all than face the embarrassment of walking in late. When I realize I'm running more than a half hour behind, I sometimes just call and cancel," she says.

Perception #2: A Control Thing

Certainly, there are those who use lateness as a way of asserting control over another person or as a way of competing for power.

They tend, however, to be in the minority. Those who do use lateness as a form of control often find arriving early to be somewhat demeaning. Arriving late allows them to feel in command of something, even if it's just the time the meeting starts.

Perception #3: "You Don't Value My Time"

While interviewing early birds, I often heard the comment, "Late people don't value my time," or "they just don't care about making others wait." Indeed, there does appear to be two camps among tardy folks—those who are troubled by their lateness, and those who have a more lackadaisical attitude about punctuality. For the most part, however, I found that late people really do try to show up on time. Lateness rarely has to do with not valuing another's time or an uncaring attitude, but more often with the inability to control one's own time.

Perception #4: Procrastination/Time Management

Are tardy people just bad time managers? Is it simply a matter of being more organized and efficient and procrastinating less? My research shows that, in general, the punctually challenged do tend to procrastinate more than the average person and often embrace a kind of determined optimism when it comes to the clock.

Many of my clients have benefited from improving their time perception and scheduling skills. In Cures Two, Three and Four, you'll find exercises to improve your time management skills and tips on overcoming procrastination.

Perception #5: Slackers

Could it be that we're just too lazy to get up and out the door? Are we snooze button punchers?

Bill Clinton is among the most famous of late people, yet he graduated with honors from Harvard Law School, achieved the status of Rhodes Scholar, held two terms as governor of Arkansas and completed two terms as president of one of the most complex industrialized nations in the world. While a certain lackadaisical attitude can be found in a number of late folks, certainly it can't account for all.

Perception #6: Bad Morale

Chronic employee lateness is often attributed to what psychologists call withdrawal behavior—in other words, bad morale. Of course, this premise has validity—sometimes. However, research indicates that most people are remarkably consistent in their punctuality styles. They're either always early or always late, regardless of whether the event is a party or a funeral. Certainly, a poor attitude can have an effective on timeliness, but more often, the cause is something deeper.

A case in point is Mike, a forty-six year old economics professor at a university in Chicago. He's dedicated to his job and has a wonderful rapport with his students. Yet, every day Mike is at least ten minutes late for each of his classes. Mike loves his job, looks forward to each day and insists bad morale has nothing to do with his trouble with time.

So What Is It, Really?

These days, most psychologists agree that habitual lateness is a symptom of subconscious motivations or complex issues. These underlying conditions not only cause tardiness, but also play a role in other problems and habits as well. In the following chapters, you'll learn more about the different types of late people and their motivations.

Most chronically late people fall into one, and frequently two or more, of the following categories:

- The Rationalizer
- The Producer
- The Deadliner
- The Indulger

- The Absent-minded Professor
- The Rebel
- The Evader

As mentioned before, you may find yourself fitting into more than one category. While many people relate to the Deadliner, for example, nearly everyone finds some aspect of themselves in the Producer as well. So please read through each chapter, even those that don't at first glance seem pertinent.

When you've finished reading the individual cures, browse through Appendix A which reviews some of the most popular exercises in the previous chapters. As you read, highlight the ideas that hit home for you. Once you've identified your lateness types and chosen your specific exercises, change is only a few steps away.

PART TWO

7 CURES FOR THE PUNCTUALLY CHALLENGED

CURE ONE

Who Me?
Face the Facts

The human capacity for self-deception is very impressive, often showing breathtaking flights of creativity.

—Jerry L. Horner,
Daniel Seligman Research Associate

"*My ability to repeatedly arrive exactly ten minutes late to meetings sixty or seventy miles away is uncanny,*" *says Bill, a sales manager for a softwaret company in Los Angeles. While his tardiness drives those around him to distraction, Bill doesn't see it as a problem. "It's really no big deal," he insists. And although he's accomplished a great deal in his career, Bill has found himself in some peculiar predicaments because of his tardiness.*

"*One day last year as I rushed to a meeting with a potential client, I mercilessly tailgated a slow moving car in front of me. After several minutes of bumper riding, horn honking and headlight flashing, the other driver pulled over to let me pass. A few minutes later, as I pulled into the client's parking lot, I noticed the other car pulling in behind me. Hurrying to the conference room, I began setting up for the presentation, but stopped in my tracks when the door opened and in walked the driver of the other car. As it turned out, this was my prospective client. After everyone had been seated, the woman turned to me and asked, 'Do you drive a black Audi SUV?'*

"Trying my best to look innocent, I replied, 'No, why?' at which point one of my colleagues, looking at me quizzically, insisted, 'Yes, you do.'

"'No, it's ahh ... gray,' I stammered. The subject was dropped, but I never did land the account."

—As told by Bill

Have you ever arrived late to meet a friend for dinner, and upon sinking into your chair, began recounting the travails of your journey—the accident on the freeway, the Federal Express truck blocking your driveway (the last being not exactly true, but you did see a truck heading down your block, which gave you the idea)?

Perhaps your friend had been waiting fifteen minutes, was livid, and began reading you the riot act. At first you apologized, but then start getting defensive. "Why is fifteen minutes such a big deal? Besides, I really did try to make it on time." Maybe you even got angry with her, grumbling, "You're really too uptight about time. In fact, people in general need to mellow out."

We've all run through these thoughts in our minds. No one likes acknowledging that they've been inconsiderate or selfish. In fact, during the course of interviewing people for this book, I noticed a trend—when it comes to the clock, late folks have an unshakable ability to engage in the fine art of rationalization.

What is rationalization? It's the man who's late to work every day but doesn't think he has a problem; the woman who points to the kids, a broken watch and the transit system for her battle with the hour.

At times, rationalization comes in quite handy, leading us to believe we're more considerate, more responsible, even better looking than we really are. In fact, if it weren't for those rose-colored glasses, reality might be pretty hard on our self-esteem. Rationalization, however, is a bit of a double-edged sword. While it helps protect our self-image, it also hampers our ability to beat bad habits.

Even if you've taken full responsibility for your tardiness and have resolved to mend your ways, rationalization may poke its head out from time-to-time to interfere with your progress. This chapter is designed to help you maintain clear thinking when it comes to time.

Are You a Rationalizer?

- Are you frequently late for work, appointments or social engagements, yet feel lateness isn't a problem?
- Do you believe people are too uptight about punctuality?
- Do you often attribute your lateness to circumstances beyond your control?
- Do you make up excuses when you're late?

If you answered yes to one or more of these questions, you may be a Rationalizer. In the following pages, you'll see how rationalization can make you late and find exercises to help beat the habit. You'll also discover the three most common traps.

Trap #1: Denying There's a Problem

Bill, the software sales manager you met earlier, insists he's late only occasionally, so it isn't a problem for him. But friends, family and colleagues tell a different story, citing missed planes, forfeited dinner reservations and frustrating delays. If Bill's situation sounds familiar—those around you complain, but you're wondering what the fuss is about—you may have a problem to which you're having difficulty admitting.

Why is it so hard for us to see our own failings and imperfections? Our minds have a natural ability to ignore information that makes us feel bad about ourselves. It's as though we each have our own internal spin doctor. When we do something irresponsible or inconsiderate, our PR guy steps in to perform damage control. "You don't have a problem with lateness," he insists. "Besides, wasn't Jane late for lunch that day last month?" Even the most critically honest of us have PR people on staff, busily spinning positive angles to our transgressions.

Another way we distance ourselves from our crimes is to accuse the person waiting of being too uptight about time. "People are too rigid," our PR friend tells us when we're chastised. For those of us who are rarely on the waiting end of the game, it's hard to see how ten or fifteen minutes is such a big deal. But as you saw in Chapter Two, when friends and colleagues are kept waiting on a regular basis, it becomes like a loan never repaid.

Trap #2: Blaming Outside Influences

In 1979, two psychological researchers named Ross & Sicoly discovered a phenomenon they referred to as "attribution theory"—the tendency of us humans to distance ourselves from our negative behavior, but to take full responsibility when things go right. That tendency accounts for this second trap.

Mike, the university professor, always has a good reason for being late to his 8:00 a.m. class—he swears it's the traffic or the student who interrupted him on his way to class. Rebecca, a housewife, says, "Of course I'm always late. I have two children to feed and dress in the morning and a household to run."

Like many of us, Mike and Rebecca blame their tardiness on external circumstances even when those same circumstances occur every day. Mike says it's the traffic, but he drives the same route and encounters the same tie-ups every morning. Rebecca attributes it to the kids, but each day she faces the same two children. Unquestionably, traffic and kids can muddle anyone's schedule, but if the same factors occur day after day, perhaps there's something more at play.

The problem with excuses is that sometimes we succeed in convincing ourselves that we really aren't to blame. Just as we often hear of celebrities who "believe their own PR," when we rationalize to the people around us, we rationalize to ourselves. Before we know it, we've fooled ourselves into thinking that we're really not at fault, but rather victims of circumstances beyond our control.

Trap #3: Minimizing the Selfishness of the Act

"I'm not a selfish person!" Devon insists. A copywriter in New York City, Devon is, in fact, a kind, caring person. Yet he shows up late to work, holds up meetings and keeps others waiting in restaurants. Because he's never late on purpose, Devon doesn't think of his chronic tardiness as a selfish act. When he consistently puts his own needs before his commitments to others, however, he is, in a sense, acting selfishly.

Sometimes we're able to minimize the selfishness of our acts because we're not called to task. The people we leave waiting don't usually enjoy the unpleasant task of scolding us, so they swallow their anger, smile graciously and accept our excuses. This allows us to blithely continue on our course, believing we really haven't caused much of a nuisance.

How did all this rationalization begin? Of course, it's not the same for everyone. Often, however, the tendency to don rose-colored glasses starts in childhood. The sensitive, anxious or shy child who is uneasy about life can take on a tendency toward deceptive thinking. In other cases, it's based on a particularly unhappy childhood, in which wishful thinking can give the child a sense of relief from the reality of his everyday world.

OVERCOMING RATIONALIZATION

How can you learn to overcome rationalization? The following steps are a start:

- Recognize the problem
- Face the consequences of your lateness
- Change your attitude

Recognize The Problem

As you learned earlier in this chapter, it's difficult to overcome negative habits if you aren't completely honest with yourself. Yet being brutally honest often goes against our natural instinct to protect our self-image. The remedy for this is to engage in a little introspection. The following exercises are intended to help you take an objective look at what you are doing and why.

Exercise One

Make an honest and straightforward inventory of your past actions. Recall and write down the occasions you've been late when the consequences were the most adverse. Try to remember as many embarrassing, agonizing and regretful moments you can—the traffic tickets, the reprimands, the missed opportunities. Try to relive how you felt when you were late and envision the reactions of others.

Look also for common threads—are you typically late across all activities, or are there certain functions for which you tend to be late most often?

Missing a flight or arriving late to a dinner party can be excruciating at the time, but for most of us, it takes only a few days to forget about the incident. Candidly recalling and writing down your experiences can help you see things with clearer eyes.

Exercise Two

Start keeping track on a daily basis of how often you are early, on time or late. Purchase a wall, computer or phone calendar and note each day whether you were late or punctual and by how many minutes. At the end of the month, add up all the incidents in each category. This will give you an accurate feel for the extent of your problem and a sense for where you need to improve.

Exercise Three

If you've acknowledged that you have a problem, the next step is to look at to what extent it is within your control. Start digging. Take a close look at your answers in Exercise One and ask yourself whether your lateness is preventable. If you're consistently late for the same activity, is there anything you can do differently? For instance, Mike says that he gets stopped in the hall on the way to class, causing him to be late. If this consistently happens, perhaps he should begin to plan for interruptions.

Facing the Consequences of Your Lateness

As you've seen, many of us are able to rationalize our problems because those left waiting don't confront us—they simply grit their teeth and continue waiting. Whether they're trying to spare our feelings or avoid an unpleasant scene, many people shy away from letting us know their thoughts.

Exercise One

Talk with a trusted friend, associate or family member about your lateness. Ask for their input and request that they be completely honest in their opinions of how your lateness impacts them. Does it cause them to lose respect for you? Most people will try to spare your feelings, and that's fine. You're looking for honesty, but not brutal honesty. Do urge them, however, to be as forthright and candid as possible.

Exercise Two

Make a deal with your friends and family members. Inform them that if you're not on time, you'll pay for wine or dessert or that they should go on without you. Of course, there will be times when this won't be possible or when doing so will inconvenience them. In that case, let those close to you know that they shouldn't ignore your tardiness, but rather feel free to address the issue.

Also encourage those around you to support your progress. Let them know that their positive feedback motivates you and further encourages your good behavior.

Exercise Three

Reward yourself. Begin to pay attention to how you feel when you're on time or early. For most people, there is a big difference— they're less harried and stressed and more confident. Paying attention to these positive feelings can serve as an incentive in itself.

Using the calendar you created in Exercise One, write down one reward you'll give yourself each week that you've maintained consistent punctuality. When you're successful, treat yourself to a nice dinner, massage, pedicure or slice of cake.

Changing Your Attitude

Understand that lateness is a choice and the choices we make are directly related to our beliefs and our way of looking at things. When you change your attitude about reliability and punctuality, your actions will, in turn, change as well.

Exercise One

Consciously change your thoughts about punctuality. Banish any lackadaisical feelings on the subject, and acknowledge to yourself that lateness is a "big deal." Don't allow yourself to underestimate the importance of living up to your commitments.

The next time you're tempted to pass off your lateness lightly, consider how you would feel if a friend or spouse consistently broke his promises to you or regularly treated you inconsiderately.

Exercise Two

Begin to increase your focus on other people and what they may be thinking or feeling. As you saw earlier, most of us aren't intentionally rude, just simply unaware of the extent to which our actions affect other people. Being aware of and caring about other people's frustrations and problems is one of the factors in increasing your sensitivity.

As you prepare to leave the house or office, envision the person or people on the other end. Imagine how they will feel and how the encounter will go if you're late. For example, if you're meeting a friend for coffee, visualize her at the cafe. It's past the appointed time, you're late, and it's not just her coffee that's steaming. Imagine her frustration and anger. See yourself sprinting though the cafe door, hair flying, making excuses.

Now imagine the opposite scenario—you've arrived at the cafe ahead of time and are sitting calmly at a table smiling when your friend walks in the door. She's pleased you're on time and you're both happy and relaxed. Play these scenarios over in your mind each time you need to be somewhere.

Exercise Three

Admit when you're late and apologize. Don't turn the tables on the other person and become angry because they're peeved with you. Apologize sincerely, explain that you're honestly striving to change your habits, and commit to doing better next time.

Exercise Four

Don't make up excuses. Remember that when you let your spin doctor take control, you run the risk of believing your own P.R. and hampering your ability to change.

Acknowledging and taking responsibility for lateness is the first step in overcoming the habit. When you begin to change your attitude about punctuality, monitor your habits and face the consequences of your actions, you'll find your on-time arrivals gradually increasing and the relationships with those around you improving as well.

REVIEW

- Many people rationalize their lateness by attributing it to factors beyond their control or by minimizing the selfishness of the act. Yet in failing to acknowledge and take responsibility for our actions, we hamper efforts to improve.

- Make an honest review of your past actions and begin to monitor your punctuality on a wall or electronic calendar.

- Discuss the problem with a trusted friend or family member and ask for honest feedback.

- Reward yourself for any progress you make, however small.

- Practice focusing on other people—what they might be thinking and feeling and how your actions affect them.

- Consciously change your attitude about punctuality. Begin to think of lateness as a promise broken or as a loan unpaid.

CURE TWO

Beat the Busy Syndrome

Nothing is easier than being busy, and nothing more difficult than being effective.

—Alec MacKenzie, time-management expert

Kim is busy—very busy. A mother of three and a part-time teacher, she also serves as head of her neighborhood social committee and as a volunteer in her children's school. She's often so over-scheduled and pressed for time, she finds herself running late or unable to properly prepare for meetings and events. Important details are overlooked and phone calls are frequently left unreturned. "I've just been so swamped lately," Kim is often heard explaining. But deep down, she likes it this way. She loves being busy and gets a sense of satisfaction and purpose as she rushes to meetings and jogs through the house, cell phone in hand, cleaning, organizing, exercising and trying to squeeze as much activity as she can into each moment. Unfortunately, all this activity can backfire.

"Last July, I threw a party for my son's tenth birthday, inviting fifteen children and their parents. Unfortunately, I inadvertently scheduled it on a day when I'd also planned a parent teacher meeting and a doctor appointment. By the time I pulled into my driveway, I faced a group of angry parents and antsy kids. 'I'm so sorry I'm late,' I pled. 'I've just got to unload these groceries and we'll be all set.'

"To distract the children while I prepared lunch, I rounded them into the family room and put in a DVD of what I thought was the latest Disney movie. As the parents and I arranged the food and tableware in the dining room, I happened to overhear the voices of the children. 'Gross!' 'Oh man!' Popping my head into the family room, I saw a dreadful site. Gathered around the TV were fifteen children intently watching a video of the birth of my youngest child. Horrified and embarrassed, I hit the stop button and announced, 'Who wants cake?' Needless to say, that little birthday party was the talk of the neighborhood for some time after."

—As told by Kim

Whendf you were a child, did you or someone you knew have a pet hamster? Remember how he used to mount the round wheel in the middle of the cage and run and run until he was exhausted? He looked so full of purpose and resolve. Every day he'd jump on and make the same trip to nowhere all over again. Round and round he would go, his little legs working as fast as he could will them.

Does that sound like you? Are your days packed so tightly you feel as though you're constantly on the run, short of time and frequently late? Ask yourself the following questions:

- Do I feel the need to squeeze as much activity as I can into each day?
- Do I view unproductive time as time "wasted"?
- Am I pleased when the day goes by quickly?
- Do I often underestimate everyday tasks, such as getting dressed in the morning or driving to work, even though I've performed those routines many times before?

If you answered yes to two or more of these questions, you may be a Producer. This chapter will help you to tame the hamster within and become a more calm, yet still productive person.

The Busy Syndrome

"If I just hurry, I can…" is a common refrain among producers. They're in a constant race with the clock to get as much done in as little time as possible and to fill their days with productive activity. They see unproductive time as "wasted" time, so they schedule their days to avoid down time, leaving no leeway for unexpected events, no room for things that might take longer than anticipated.

Producers never plan to be early. Instead, they try to time things so that they're exactly on time. Arriving early and having to wait is akin to squandering a precious resource, letting time slip through their fingers. If the drive to work takes twenty minutes and it's twenty-two minutes before 9:00 a.m., do they leave the house? Are you kidding? They have two whole minutes. If they hurry, they can still take out the garbage, clean the bathtub or change the battery in the smoke detector. Although they're simply trying to be as efficient as possible, all this "productivity" and split-second timing leaves them under the gun and behind schedule.

Magical Thinking

Ami is an architect in San Francisco. She heads up a staff of ten and brings home a salary well into six digits. She's been a competitive swimmer, an honors student in college and an amateur photographer, but she's also habitually late.

"Last week I arranged to meet a man I'll call Dylan for a lunch date at a restaurant downtown. I had a few appointments earlier that morning and finished the last one at eleven-thirty, plenty of time to meet him at noon. As I left the building, I looked at my watch and realized I had just enough time to pop into a department store to look for new linens for an upcoming dinner party. Well, things took a little longer than I expected, and the next thing I knew, it was noon. I called Dylan to say I'd be late, and he seemed OK about it. On the drive to the restaurant, I happened to glance down and see that my nail polish was chipped. "It'll only take a minute," I said to myself. So I rushed home and painted my nails. By the time I finally arrived at the restaurant, Dylan was so mad, his face was bright red. I don't know what made me think I had time to go home and paint my nails, but I just thought if I hurried..."

Like many producers, Ami is a "magical thinker"—an eternal optimist who consistently overestimates how much she can accomplish in a specific period of time. Because of her drive to get as much done as possible, Ami idealizes the time each of her tasks will take. She convinces herself she can choose linens in ten minutes, drive across town in five and paint her nails in two. Even when her watch says she should leave *now*, Ami is certain she can squeeze in one more thing and still get to where she's going on time. Does this sound familiar?

Like Ami, you may be overly optimistic when it comes to judging time. You make long, ambitious lists of things to do, then find the hands on the clock have moved faster than you thought possible. As time runs out, you attempt to play catch up, rushing ever faster and assuring yourself that if you just hurry, you'll accomplish all you set out to do (and maybe more).

Of the hundreds of late people I've interviewed, nearly all have said, "I always seem to underestimate the amount of time it takes to get somewhere." You may even misjudge those things you do every day, like driving to work. If once eight years ago, you made it in fifteen minutes, somehow fifteen minutes becomes ingrained in your mind. From that day forward, you allot exactly fifteen minutes to get to work. You forget that on that fine day back in history, you encountered no traffic, hit all the green lights and found parking in front of the building. Yet fifteen minutes is firmly implanted in your mind.

In a recent seminar I conducted on the subject of lateness, I met a young couple I'll call Derik and Grace. Before they were married, Grace had given Derik an ultimatum, refusing to marry him until he could manage to be on time for two months in a row. After many false starts, Derik finally made it through the two months and they were married. Shortly after the wedding, however, Derik lapsed back into his old habits and Grace was at her wit's end.

Midway through my presentation, an amazed look came over Derik's face. Raising his hand excitedly, he exclaimed, "I just had an ah ha moment!" He went on to explain that when he was eight years-old, his father had offered him three dollars if he could get ready for football practice in seven minutes. Rushing madly through the house, throwing off clothes and suiting up in his uniform, Derik made it within the deadline and collected his three dollars. During my talk, Derik realized that since that fateful day, he'd given himself precisely seven minutes to get ready for work and social events. Seven minutes was implanted in his mind.

How is it that some of us are able to consistently misjudge time? While the desire to stay busy and productive accounts for part of the equation, another factor may be the "right-brain dominance" theory, based on Nobel Prize recipient Dr. Roger Sperry's research on the two hemispheres of the brain. His research indicates that in most people, the right brain is responsible for intuitive and creative characteristics, while the left side produces organizational talents, including the ability to accurately gauge time. Dr. Sperry theorized that while everyone uses both hemispheres of the brain simultaneously, most people naturally depend on one hemisphere more than the other. Hence, those who are "right-brain dominant" may have more difficulty estimating time.

A third scenario, suggests psychologist Neil Fiore, Ph.D., author of *The Now Habit*, is one in which a child experiences an overly indulgent childhood and enters adulthood embracing a kind of "all things possible" attitude ignoring the natural laws of time and space. This is what is often referred to as a Peter Pan Syndrome, one in which adults resist growing up and facing the limitations of the real world. Peter Panners have a tendency to see the world and their surroundings as they would like them to be, rather than the way they really are.

Getting it all Done

What causes this passion for busyness and productivity? Certainly, it feels good to be industrious, and when you've accomplished a great deal in a day, your ego gets a boost; you feel competent and effective. What's more, our culture places a great deal of importance on efficiency and accomplishment. There's a clear message that busy people are important people, even those who are obviously overcommitted and spread too thin. Writer Adair Lara calls this "artificial urgency":

> *"It's the feeling that time is to be used efficiently and productively. Even though, you know really, that means if you can balance three spinning plates on sticks, you're rewarded with a fourth, then a fifth."*

A growing phenomenon throughout the world today seems to be an ever-increasing emphasis on achievement and competition. Ironically, many of us complain about the lack of hours in a day, but then say we love being busy because it "makes the day go by faster." But why do we want the day to go by fast? What are we racing toward? Shouldn't we be savoring each moment rather than living our lives like a contest, where the winner is the person who's accomplished the most in the least amount of time?

What's more, no matter how fast we run, we still end up feeling guilty about the things we didn't do. Sooner or later it catches up to us. In a survey by the National Recreation and Parks Association, 38 percent of people reported feeling "too busy," with working mothers topping the charts at a whopping 64 percent.

While we might grumble about being swamped, many of us forget that we've elected this path, chosen to pile our plates high with nonstop action, never slowing down long enough to breathe much less consider what we're doing. The late author Richard Carlson, in his best-selling book *Don't Sweat The Small Stuff… And It's All Small Stuff,* said it well:

> *"So many of us live our lives as if the secret purpose is to somehow get everything done. We stay up late, get up early, avoid having fun, and keep our loved ones waiting… Often, we convince ourselves that our obsession with our "to-do" list is only temporary—that once we get through the list, we'll be calm, relaxed, and happy. But in reality, this rarely happens. As items are checked off, new ones simply replace them.…"*

In a trip to Italy with friends, I had an unexpected opportunity to spend a few days alone in Rome. Striking up a conversation with a waiter during dinner one evening, we talked about the differences between Italians and Americans. "In Italy," Paulo said "we have the impression that Americans work too hard." At the time, I laughed and continued on with my meal, thinking, "Yes, but look at all we've accomplished." While browsing through shops and lounging in piazzas over the next few days, however, I couldn't help but notice the gusto with which the Italians appeared to enjoy life. I watched as old men chatted with neighbors and young couples huddled over vino in outdoor cafes. I came back to America with a niggling feeling that perhaps we had accomplished a great deal, but at what cost?

While staying busy and on the run may feel good, it sometimes keeps us so occupied, we lose sight of our long-term goals and priorities. Instead of thoughtfully planning our days, we follow whatever direction the day takes us and do whatever's in front of us. We're reactive rather than proactive. Reacting is more natural and easier because we don't have to think, we can just do.

When we live in a reactive way, however, we forget to make time for the important things in life. We neglect picnics with the children, dinners by candlelight and evenings watching the sunset. Our goal is to be efficient and productive, rather than relaxed and happy.

No matter how good it feels to be productive, sacrificing your sanity, not to mention the respect of others, is counterproductive in the long run. Remember, life is not about how much you accomplish, but rather about whether you accomplished the right things.

In this chapter, you'll learn how to beat the busy syndrome, how to find time for the important things in life and ways to embrace a well-balanced schedule.

BEATING THE BUSY SYNDROME

Think of many things. Do one.

— Portuguese saying

Does escaping the productivity trap sound appealing, if perhaps a little unrealistic? Beating the busy syndrome is not so much about slowing down as it is about prioritizing how you use your time, remembering your goals and spending time on things that really matter. There are three things that will help you accomplish this:

- Stop squeezing so much into each day.
- Don't confuse "waiting time" with "wasted time."
- Overcome magical thinking.

Stop Squeezing so Much into Each Day

Each day, we face a myriad of things to do, tasks we're sure must be done—washing the car, picking up the dry cleaning, returning phone calls and so on. But trying to pack everything into today leads to mindless rushing and contributes to lateness. The following exercises will help you to relax, pace yourself and be more realistic about what you attempt on any given day.

Exercise One

Create a mantra to curb your optimism. Instead of saying, "If I hurry, I can ...," slow down for a few minutes, take a deep breath and think about what you're doing. Then repeat one of the following mantras:

- "Am I being realistic or optimistic?
- "Am I doing too much?"
- "Is this something I really need to do now?

Let's say you're writing a memo and, glancing at the clock, notice you're running short of time to get to an appointment. Typically, you would give in to the temptation to finish the memo, convincing yourself that if you just wrote faster, you'd finish and still get to the meeting on time. From now on, give yourself a midstream wake-up call either by taking a deep breath or by performing a quick physical act such as clapping your hands or tapping your foot. Then repeat one of the mantras. You'll usually find that small acts will help you to make the right decision rather than acting on impulse.

Jeff Davidson, in his book *The Complete Idiot's Guide to Managing Stress*, recommends repeating the mantra, "What's the worst thing that will happen if I don't do this?" The answer will probably be nothing. If you leave the house without making the bed, will your mother-in-law unexpectedly turn up? Probably not. If you go to work without washing your hair, will anyone really notice? Envisioning the worst case scenario will help keep things in perspective.

Throughout this book, you'll find suggested mantras for working through lateness and procrastination. Special words and phrases have an amazing ability to help clear our heads and make conscious choices about our activities and our lives.

Exercise Two

Learn to say no to others. For many of us, trying to fulfill others' needs or expectations comes as second nature. Even when our time is stretched to the breaking point, it can be difficult to turn down requests. Rather than having to disappoint or deal with unfavorable reactions, it's often easier just to say yes. But just as you've learned the importance of saying no to yourself, you can learn to say no to others. Having a set of answers will help you consciously choose your most important commitments. Following are a few to try:

- "I'm sorry, but I'm already overcommitted."
- "Thanks, but I'll have to pass on that."
- "Thanks for thinking of me, but I already have plans."

Once you've said no, don't give in to the need to explain any further or apologize unnecessarily. You'll probably find that once you've stated your decision, most people will accept your answer. If they continue to press, simply repeat your mantra again.

Don't Confuse "Waiting Time" with "Wasted Time"

As you've seen, many of us are adverse to arriving early to our destinations because we view waiting as time wasted. We plan our arrivals to the minute so that we'll arrive exactly on time. An important key to overcoming tardiness is changing that just-in-time mentality. Recognize that waiting is not such a terrible thing, but rather, a guilt-free time to relax and enjoy life.

Exercise One

Never plan to be exactly on-time. Always plan to be early. If you try to arrive precisely on-time, I can promise you'll be late more often than not. Something will always take longer than expected or some unanticipated wrench will be thrown in your path.

Vince Lombardi, former coach of the Greenbay Packers used to insist that his players and staff arrive fifteen minutes prior to practice or meetings. Everyone knew this as "Lombardi Time," and adhered to it religiously. Incorporate this 15-minute early philosophy into your own life. You'll usually find that doing so will actually get you there right on time.

If leaving the house or office before the last possible moment is difficult for you, try this trick: Whenever you prepare to go somewhere, plan to take time to do something enjoyable but unnecessary right before you're scheduled to leave. For example, when I have dinner plans and need to leave the house by 6:30, I'll plan to be ready by 6:15 so I can practice the piano for a few minutes before I leave. Invariably, I run behind and find that I don't have time for piano practice. But scheduling in those extra minutes gives me just the right amount of spare time I need to get to dinner on time.

Exercise Two

Welcome the wait. When you begin to arrive on-time or early, you may be the one who has to wait. Don't think of those extra minutes as waiting time. Instead, think of waiting as luxury time, time to engage in something fun or to catch up on things for which you don't normally have time. Instead of squirming impatiently while waiting at the doctor's office, sit down and relax. You probably wouldn't otherwise find the time for your own personal recess, so enjoy it! When you give your wait a different label, you'll learn to welcome the delay.

Of course, you may not have had a great deal of experience with waiting. But if you are going to win the punctuality game, you'll be doing a bit more waiting than you used to. So learn to take pleasure in it.

Exercise Three

Prepare for the wait. Remember how your mother brought along books and toys for you to play with on the plane or at the doctor's office? It kept you from getting cranky and fussy while you waited. Well, we're not really so far removed from those cantankerous kids. If we're going to learn to welcome the wait, we'll need things to distract us, to keep us entertained while we wait.

Come prepared with something interesting to do. Start thinking now about what might keep you occupied. Consider writing that thank-you card, listening to a podcast or reading an article on investments for your IRA. Following are a few more ideas that may help make waiting a pleasurable experience.

- Bring a book, magazine or article to read.
- Catch up on your emails, texts and phone calls.
- Start planning where to go on your next vacation.
- Brainstorm on how to solve a particular problem or dilemma.
- Strike up a conversation with a stranger.
- Write a letter to a friend or relative.
- People watch.
- Make a list of activities for the coming weekend.
- Make a list of restaurants you'd like to visit and plays or movies you'd like to see.
- Make a list of hobbies or skills you'd like to try.

- Use a phone app or other electronic device to hone your chess or bridge game.
- Use a language app to learn a foreign-language.
- Practice deep breathing exercises.

Exercise Four

While you're waiting, don't agonize over all the things you could or should be doing. Don't allow yourself to pace, sigh loudly, drum your fingers or look at your watch every few minutes. Whether you're waiting for a friend, colleague or client, once you've arrived, there's usually little you can do about the delay, so don't torment yourself about "wasting time." Now that you're committed to being a timely, reliable person, some waiting will be inevitable. The more gracious you are, the happier you'll be.

Remember Kim, the woman who was always on a fast track to somewhere? Well, she's actually gotten used to waiting and even looks forward to it. She's found so much enjoyment in guilt-free relaxing that she finds herself disappointed when she doesn't have to wait. "I've come to welcome the pause in my fast-paced day as a time-out to read, relax and just think. Without the enforced break, I would probably never take time to stop and enjoy downtime, but now I look forward to it," Kim says.

Overcoming Magical Thinking

As you've seen, many latecomers have a very different concept of time—engaging in a kind of magical thinking by underestimating how much time their tasks will take. The following exercises will help you overcome any magical thinking tendencies of your own.

Exercise One

Relearn how to tell time. Time management studies indicate the average chronically late person underestimates by twenty-five to thirty-five percent how much time a given task will require. Because we base our time estimates on something that happened long ago, we tend to miscalculate the same tasks day-after-day.

Start by listing all the fixed daily or weekly events that make up your schedule, such as driving to work or class, grocery shopping, getting dressed and so on. Although your list may be as detailed or as general as you'd like, the more detail you provide, the easier it will be for you to see where you're misjudging your time. Across from each entry, jot down how long you think it takes to accomplish the task. Following is an example:

Shower and get dressed	40 minutes
Straighten house	15 minutes
Eat breakfast	20 minutes
Gather briefcase, keys, books	5 minutes
Drive to work	25 minutes
Write monthly reports	60 minutes
Prepare for staff meeting	40 minutes
Pick up kids at school	30 minutes
Grocery shop	45 minutes
Drive to art class	10 minutes

Next, determine how accurate your perceptions of time are. Over the next two weeks, keep track of how long each activity actually took. Be sure to keep track every day because it's important to determine the worst-case scenario, the time it takes when things go wrong. Does it really take forty minutes to take a shower and get dressed, or is it closer to an hour? How long is your commute on a bad day?

As you complete this stage, you will probably be surprised at how long things really take and you'll start to become more realistic about your time as a result.

Finally, take your new time estimates and add in time for contingencies. Build in leeway for things that might go wrong or that may take longer than expected.

From now on, incorporate specific, concrete schedules into your daily life using your new time estimates. Schedule your day as you would if you were a doctor or dentist, with time slots and estimates for each activity. When you're definite and precise in your everyday life, you'll be more realistic and in better control of your time.

Exercise Two

Learn to work with phone or digital alarms to stay on track. Just as an alarm helps you to get out of bed in the morning, so can it help you get out the door. Using your new time estimates, set your alarm to go off 10 minutes prior to the time you need to leave. When it rings, that's your cue to finish up and walk out.

An alternative to using a timer is make use of music. Put on a favorite CD and determine which song is your "ten-minute warning." When you hear that tune, you'll know it's time to start wrapping things up.

Timers and music serve as good reality checks, audible reminders that time is marching on. If you practice this habit for one week, you'll begin to recognize and adapt to "real time" and be less likely to slip into "magical time."

As you work through the exercises in this chapter, try to remember that it's not how much you get done that is important, but whether or not you focused on the right things. By learning to curb your optimism, welcome the wait and relearn to tell time, you'll not only overcome lateness, but also gain perspective and learn to slow down and enjoy life.

REVIEW

- Being busy and productive reassures us and boosts our self-esteem. Consistently over-scheduling, however, causes us to forget our goals and focus on less important activities in life.

- Try to curb your optimism about how many activities you can or should squeeze into each day. When you're tempted to add one last task before leaving the house or office, stop and repeat your mantra.
- Change your attitude toward "wasted" time and "waiting" time. Begin to think of waiting time as luxury time.
- Never plan to be exactly on time. Always plan to be early. Doing so will usually get you there just in time.
- Schedule in something completely unnecessary before leaving. This will give you some buffer time in case things take longer than you anticipated.
- Relearn to tell time by tracking the time it really takes to complete your daily activities.
- Stay on track by using music or alarms.

CURE THREE

Get Off the Rollercoaster

Without a deadline baby, I wouldn't do nothin'.

—Duke Ellington

"My grandfather, Homer Duggenfinger, was an admired and highly respected member of the First Baptist Church in Durham, North Carolina. Everyone knew Grandpa for his kindness, generous contributions and active participation in church affairs. He was a born leader—chairing committees, leading children's and adult's prayer groups and speaking at Sunday church services.

"As well-known as Grandpa was for his leadership and charitable activities, he was equally famous for being late. Many a Sunday morning, my grandmother would arrive for 9:30 services, her five *children in tow but noticeably missing Grandpa, who would typically sneak in somewhere around 10:00. While his tardiness wasn't usually much of a nuisance, there were times when he was scheduled to address the congregation, yet could nowhere be found. Grandma says that on those occasions, folks would sit fidgeting in their seats, restlessly waving paper fans in the hot air and training their eyes on the rear doors of the church. Eventually, Grandpa would come bursting through the entry, Bible in hand and make his way up to the pulpit, nodding and smiling along the way.*

"When Grandpa died at age eighty-five, there was a grand memorial service and nearly two hundred people came to pay their respects. Grandma says that after everyone was seated and the sniffles had died down, Dr. Knight, the longtime minister of First Baptist, stepped to the podium to address the congregation. Solemnly clearing his throat, he looked down upon Grandpa's casket. 'Well, one thing I can say for Homer,' he announced, 'In the fifty years I've known him, I'll wager this is the first occasion he's been on time for church.'"

—Mrs. Betty Duggenfinger, Durham, North Carolina

Among the various types of competitions in the world of equestrian riding are two jumping events: hunters and jumpers. In the hunter division, riders and their horses complete a series of eight or more jumps, attempting to appear as calm, graceful and aesthetically pleasing as possible. To win, a horse must take off and land in just the right spots and execute perfect arcs over each fence.

The jumper division, on the other hand, is an exciting, fast-paced event in which riders and their horses complete a course of jumps as quickly as possible. Contestants gallop around, frantically turning and skidding toward the finish line. It doesn't matter what they look like, just how fast they can run when the clock is ticking. Those who complete the ride in the least amount of time, knocking down the fewest rails, win the event. Jumper classes take a certain kind of rider to handle the stress—the kind of person who thrives on adrenaline.

While jumpers is an exciting event, it bears mentioning that riders in this class crash more often and suffer more serious injuries as a result. Their horses frequently come up lame and regularly sustain damage to tendons and ligaments. Yet even with all the downsides, most jumper riders wouldn't give up their sport for anything.

Of hunters and jumpers, which appeals most to you? If you chose jumpers, you may be what I call a "deadliner." Like jumpers, deadliners prefer moving fast, are easily bored and enjoy a good race against the clock.

Are you a deadliner? How many of the following apply to you?

- I work best under pressure.

- I like a fast-paced life-style.

- I often have difficulty getting motivated without an impending deadline.

- I am probably more easily bored than most people.

If you saw yourself in two or more of these statements, consider yourself a deadliner—a person who seeks out excitement and stimulation, who enjoys the rush of the last minute race to the finish line. Whether you're dashing around the house before work or furiously jamming papers into your briefcase before a meeting, rushing makes you feel alive, focused and purposeful.

Deadliners typically fall into one or both of the following groups:

- Those who use adrenaline to relieve feelings of anxiety or boredom

- Those who require a crisis to get motivated

51

Adrenaline Junkies

We've all heard of "adrenaline junkies," those folks who participate in various extreme sports. They bungee jump in the summer, heli-ski in the winter and skydive in the spring. Of course, you don't necessarily have to engage in dangerous activities to be a deadliner; you just have to crave stimulation. And that daily dose of stimulation can sometimes be achieved by waiting until the last minute to do things.

Adrenaline seekers are those of us who are attracted to the physiological feelings that come with running late. Life is more enjoyable when there's a feeling of urgency and we thrive under stress. Our hearts pound, adrenaline is released into our bloodstreams, we're more alert and we think more clearly. To a point, this type of stress can be a pleasant feeling. When the pressure is on, our most vital, focused side comes out and we feel alive.

Like an overtime game of basketball in which players frantically try to beat the clock, close calls create a sense of drama and excitement. The moments leading up to leaving the house can be similar to the excitement of playing the game—the suspense and the gamble of making one more play, nearly running out of time then coming through in the final moments.

There's nothing more satisfying than winning the game—getting to the meeting on time, arriving before the bride, turning in a report just under the deadline. But there's nothing worse than losing—arriving at a job interview twenty minutes late, missing a flight, limping in after the meeting's over. Unfortunately, adrenaline seekers usually end up losing more often than winning.

Understand that adrenaline seekers only subconsciously enjoy the buildup of tension caused by the last-minute push. I don't want to imply that they consciously enjoy arriving late. Nothing could be further from the truth. The idea of being reliable and responsible actually appeals to the deadliner, but the reality of getting somewhere in a calm, methodical fashion goes against his natural affinity for the fast life.

For thrill-seekers, adrenaline can be a way of staving off boredom and anxiety. While most people dislike being bored, idle time is not just unoccupied time for the deadliner; it's a source of anxiety. Creating stimulating and adrenaline-producing situations is a way of distracting him from his feelings. Rather than accepting the sometimes slowness of life, the deadliner attempts to deal with boredom and the anxiety it causes by starting fires and rushing to put them out.

Needing a Crisis to Get Motivated

Lynne, an attorney, perpetual procrastinator and inveterate late person, once wrote to me that she "needed a crisis to get motivated." She went on to describe how it all started in her college years:

"I was a horrible procrastinator in law school. I'd always begin writing papers the day before they were due and I was usually so unprepared for tests, I'd have to pull all-nighters the night before. I had such a hard time starting any earlier.

I remember one class in particular. It was a 9 a.m. class, and I had made the mistake of staking out a front row seat. I was usually at least ten minutes late because I'd be home cramming before school in the morning. I would sneak in as unobtrusively as possible, but as soon as I opened the door, Professor Marks would stop talking and start again only after I'd taken my seat. I would slink down the aisle shrinking with embarrassment.

"I guess the coup de grace came during midterms, for which I had, naturally, put off studying. I couldn't bear the thought of taking the test and failing, so I called Dr. Marks with a story that I was in the hospital with kidney stones (don't ask me where I came up with that one). I'll always remember the sound of his voice—so concerned and caring. "Don't worry about the test dear, you just take care of..." But as the words left his lips, my roommate burst into the room, yelling, "Lynne, come on, everyone is waiting for us!" I stumbled out an explanation, but I could tell he didn't

believe me.

"You'd think I would have learned my lesson in school, but now, seven years later, I still procrastinate preparing briefs and filing papers, and now instead of being late to class, I'm late to court. One judge recently threatened to hold me in contempt if I was tardy one more time."

Lynne is the type of deadliner who requires a crisis to get motivated. She explains that she works best under pressure. And it's true; when crises come up, you can always count on Lynne to jump into action. But in the absence of that pressure, she has difficulty motivating herself. Her last-minute preparations for depositions and court dates show up as just that—last minute efforts.

How often have you said, "I work best under pressure?" Sometimes it's hard for the best of us to get going. We all require some degree of necessity or stress to move forward. But for some of us, self-motivation is particularly tough. So we rely on crises to prod us along. Instead of being motivated internally, we're motivated externally. Like runners at the starting line, we're waiting for the final shot to go off. Getting a head start rarely occurs to us. Where some people might fall apart under stress, we find tension to be a great motivator.

Of course, nearly everyone admits to procrastinating to some extent. We all have times when we watch *The Today Show* instead of getting ready for work or sharpen pencils when we should be preparing for a meeting. Yet research indicates that late people, as a group, procrastinate more than most. For the timely, procrastination is a sporadic occurrence. For the late, it's a way of life. The person who consistently delays leaving the house is also likely to postpone starting an exercise program, preparing for meetings, returning phone calls or visiting relatives.

While deadlining can be an exciting sport, thrill-seekers pay for their habits in many areas. We come to meetings under-prepared, give speeches unrehearsed and generally lead frazzled lives. Although many of us have gotten quite good at mustering up the energy for the last minute push, in the long run, it works to our detriment. On the occasions we do pull off the seemingly impossible—making it to work in record time or catching that plane we were sure we'd miss—our habits are reinforced.

What Causes Deadlining?

Why all this desire for drama? Many prominent psychologists believe that deadlining, like other compulsive behaviors, is in part, a hereditary characteristic. Studies have led some to estimate that the urge to thrill-seek is approximately sixty percent due to hereditary factors.

As far back as the 1930s, psychologists such as C.J. Jung have found evidence indicating that differences in behavior are related to the basic personalities we're born with. One striking example of this is the great variety of physical differences found in the brain biochemistries of newborn infants, particularly in those areas that govern emotions and impulsiveness. Another indication of physiological ties to behavior is the research on adult identical twins separated at birth. Scientists have found notably similar temperaments and preferences such as shared talents for math or music, habits such as smoking or alcohol consumption and traits such as gregariousness or shyness.

Curiously, biologists also have found that people who crave excitement often carry a longer version of one gene on the eleventh chromosome. This gene influences the brain's response to dopamine, a chemical responsible for feelings of pleasure and euphoria, whose release may be triggered by exciting or risky experiences.

Other people simply need more stimulation than others. In a 1984 study, two psychologists named Anderson and Brown found that each individual has an optimal level of physiological base arousal. Further research suggests that thrill-seekers may actually have a lower level of base arousal, which they continually try to raise with stimulating experiences. In other words, our bodies, our minds and our need for stimulation are all different. So while Ann next door may be perfectly content to make her way through the day in a calm, collected fashion, Beth down the street isn't comfortable unless she's on the run.

OVERCOMING DEADLINING

If you enjoy a hectic, fast-paced life, it may be difficult to forego the tendency to deadline. The good news is that you don't necessarily have to give it up entirely. If you love the stimulation, the hustle and bustle, you'll only feel frustrated trying to become a calm, unhurried person. Adrenaline-seeking may simply be the temperament you were born with, and instead of trying to change it, you're better off learning to work with it.

Deadlining is not like alcoholism, where it's best to quit cold turkey. Rather, it's more like dieting, where you need merely to temper it, to learn when it's appropriate and when it's not. Following are three basic steps that will teach you to motivate yourself in everyday life and help curb the tendency to turn daily tasks into a sprint to the finish line.

- Recognize how and when you create crises in your life.
- Learn to motivate yourself in the absence of a crisis.
- Find more constructive ways to obtain stimulation.

Recognize How You Create Crises in Your Life

The first step in dealing with the tendency to deadline is to begin noticing how and when you create crises in your life and what emotions you feel in those circumstances.

Exercise One

Become aware of what I call your "automatic thoughts and actions." Automatic thoughts and actions are those you think and do every day without being fully conscious of them. Do you know, for instance, which shoe you put on first in the morning? If you're typical, you can't immediately say for sure. Do you know what activities lead up to being late? Most people aren't cognizant of these either.

Begin to pay attention to the things you do automatically. Ask yourself what actions you performed prior to being late and what situations seem to provoke them. If you see patterns, jot them down.

Exercise Two

Begin to notice your emotions when you create crises in your life. Were you bored, anxious or lethargic? If so, did creating a crisis relieve those feelings? Did you feel tension and if so, was it a pleasant feeling? Did it wake you up or help you to get motivated?

Motivating Yourself in the Absence of a Crisis

Remember this psychological principle—one of the best ways to get rid of one habit is to replace it with another. This is what is called substitution. If the adrenaline rush of hurrying motivates you, you'll need to find a different type of stimulation to provide equal encouragement to move forward.

Bear in mind that even though lateness can cause a myriad of problems in your life, you are getting something—a benefit—out of all this rushing around. First, there's the adrenaline rush, often a pleasant feeling. Second, instead of having to motivate yourself by starting your own mental motor, you're depending on crises to spur you along. Because you'll be giving up these benefits, you'll have to find another, stronger benefit for getting there early. Following are a few exercises to try.

Exercise One

Start a contest with yourself or a friend. Have a game to see if you can be ten minutes early for one week straight. Make it fun and stimulating. Write up a contract, track your progress on a wall or electronic calendar and enlist the support of your friends and family. Give yourself rewards for winning and penalties for losing. One woman's husband promised her a new set of golf clubs if she could be on time for three months in a row. Another woman gave her boyfriend a ten-minute back rub every day he managed to arrive for dinner by seven.

Exercise Two

Change your "just-in-time" mind-set. Consciously or not, most deadliners hold the iron-clad belief that it doesn't make sense to do anything until it absolutely must be done. We run our gas tanks on empty before stopping to fill up, pay our bills on the last possible day and prepare for the big presentation the night before. A big part of breaking the deadlining habit is to fundamentally change that "just-in-time" attitude.

Practice doing things ahead of time, not just in matters to do with punctuality, but in other areas of your life as well. Every day for one week, chose one task you'll do early, before it must be done. Each night, plan ahead by choosing your task for the next day.

Sometimes we put tasks off until the last minute because they seem burdensome or complicated. In those cases, try breaking the tasks down into small, manageable steps. Lao-Tzu, a famous philosopher once said, "A journey of a thousand miles must begin with a single step." When you break a difficult task down, instead of facing an overwhelmingly difficult project, you've got a series of small, easy-to-identify jobs. Starting becomes less of a challenge.

The following tasks are commonly-put-off ones that, when tackled ahead of time, can help break a just-in-time mentality:

- Fill the gas tank in your car when it gets to the halfway mark. Don't wait for the empty light to appear.
- Stop showing up at the gym, store or restaurant just before closing. When you go somewhere, go well within the hours

of operation.

- Get out of bed ten minutes earlier than you have to.

- Whether it's picking up the dry cleaning, going to the bank or shopping for groceries, do it before you've run out of clothes, money or food.

- Buy replacement items before you're out of the old ones. Don't let yourself run low on stamps, tape, staples, notepads, toothpaste, shampoo, nylons or shaving cream.

- Do your taxes, register for classes and send in your DMV renewal a month ahead.

- Go to the dentist for a preventative appointment before you get that toothache.

- Pay your bills seven days before the due dates.

- Return calls, e-mails or letters as soon as you receive them.

- Turn in a report early.

- Shop for holiday presents in November.

- When you have an important function to attend, decide what you'll wear at least four days in advance. This will give you time, to shop, mend, wash or dry clean instead of frantically looking for alternatives at the last minute.

- Eat before you're starving.

- Before going to bed each night, prepare everything you'll need for the next day. Choose your clothes, gather your books or briefcase, load the coffee-maker and find your keys. Don't wait until the workday morning to prepare.

When you gradually incorporate proactive routines into your life, you build a foundation for being motivated internally rather than externally. You begin to embrace the idea that there's usually no harm, and certainly many benefits, in doing things early. Soon this new attitude will take root and become a natural way of thinking.

Find Other Ways To Add Excitement to Your Life

People with interesting and stimulating lives are less likely to seek out thrills by deadlining. By finding other ways to keep energized and stimulated, you won't be as compelled to play "beat the clock" in your everyday life.

Exercise One:

Once each day do something different, something you wouldn't normally do. Drive a different way to work or explore a new part of town. Strike up a conversation with a stranger. Go to dinner or a movie by yourself or take up a new or exciting sport. When you take steps to make your life interesting and exciting in positive ways, you're less likely to succumb to the need to deadline.

Anyone can change from a deadliner to a calm and composed early person. But doing so may mean giving up something you're used to getting. If you've been relying on the game of "beat the clock" to get going, you'll now have to become accustomed to motivating yourself. This isn't as stimulating at first, but with practice it will eventually become a welcome part of your life.

REVIEW

- Chronic lateness can be caused by the urge for adrenaline-producing experiences or by needing a crisis to get motivated.
- Learn to recognize how and when you create crises in your life.
- Pay attention to your automatic behavior.
- Find other ways to motivate yourself with contests and games.
- Break the "just-in-time" mind-set by regularly completing daily tasks ahead of time.
- Find other ways to add stimulation to your life by doing something a bit different every day.

CURE FOUR

Develop Your Discipline Muscle

She's always late for everything, except for every meal.
—About Maria, from *The Sound of Music*

"I'll never forget my first day as a marketing representative for a financial systems firm. As I lay in bed that morning, I dawdled, listening to the birds chirp and daydreaming about my new career. It wasn't until the last possible minute that I jumped out of bed and began rushing to get ready. 'I've got to get around to changing that light bulb,' I muttered as I fumbled around in the dark bedroom closet. By that time, I was really running late, so I threw on a suit and shoes, grabbed my briefcase and ran out the door with just enough time to catch a cab downtown.

"My new manager had directed me to a large, modern office building where we were to monitor the installation of a new system for a brokerage client. Bounding up the steps, I happened to look down and froze in place at what I saw. On my right foot was a light gray

high-heeled pump with a bow perched on the toe. On my left foot was a dark gray pump, noticeably lacking a bow and sporting a significantly lower heel—different shoes from different pairs. I had left not a minute to spare. It was too late to go back home to change and too early for the stores to open.

"Just then, I spied a former colleague crossing the street in front of the building. 'Rachel,' I called out, 'I need to borrow your shoes!' Desperately, I explained the situation to her, but there was no way I could convince her to hand over those shoes. Slowly, I entered the building and rode the elevator to the tenth floor. I spent the majority of that morning artfully trying to disguise my shoe situation. I stood with one foot in front of the other, one foot behind a door, both feet behind a desk, and so on. By mid-morning I thought I'd gotten away scot-free. With just ten minutes to go before lunch, I passed a trader who had bent down to retrieve a dropped note. With his face near the floor, he paused as he took in my fashion statement. Looking up with a wide smile, he introduced himself and in a laughing voice, said, 'Nice shoes.'"
—As told by Edi

S elf-control, self-discipline, willpower—all different ways of saying the same thing: the ability to push ourselves forward, to make sacrifices, the inner strength to do what's right.

Each day we fight the battle between what we feel like doing and what we know we really should do. Once in a while we even win. We exercise self-discipline when we stumble out of bed in the morning, as we head to the gym instead of the couch after work, when we choose the pasta primavera instead of the sirloin steak and all the other times we hold our tongues, wait patiently and say please. On the other hand, sometimes it seems as if we lose the battle with our impulses just as often as we win. Those times we hit the snooze button on the alarm clock, order that high-fat dessert or break our New Year's resolutions all serve to remind us that we're not quite the highly disciplined people we'd like to be. Even when we do find the strength to do what's right, our willpower waxes and wanes on a daily basis. We report for work early on Monday and slink in half an hour late on Tuesday. We binge and diet, exercise fanatically one week and lie on the couch the next. Finding the right amount of consistent, long-term self-control is the trick that eludes so many of us.

Perhaps you're not among the Deadliners or the Producers I discussed in previous chapters. You may simply be a person who needs to build their discipline muscle. How does an undeveloped discipline muscle affect your ability to be on time? As you know, getting out the door in a prompt fashion isn't always easy. It often involves some kind of compromise, some type of choice. When you wake up in the morning, you choose between lying in bed another ten minutes and getting to work on time. As you prepare for a meeting, you choose between making one last change on the agenda and being on time. It's when you choose the easy thing—the instant gratification—over the right thing that you demonstrate a lack of self-discipline.

Think back to those times you've been late. At some point in preparing to leave, you made a choice, consciously or not, that caused you to run behind. Perhaps you decided to have an extra cup of coffee or change clothes one more time. Even though you knew you might be cutting it close, you weren't willing to make the sacrifice necessary to be on time. Learning how to make those sacrifices—to be willing to tolerate the minor discomforts that come with them—is an essential part of acquiring the discipline you'll need to be an early person. In fact, to succeed with any of the exercises in this book, you'll first need to build your discipline muscle. It's the foundation on which everything else stems.

Studies suggest that late people as a group may have more difficulty with discipline than the timely. My own research supports this—in psychological tests, the chronically tardy scored lower than timely people in self-control, while scoring higher in impulsivity. Late folks, for instance, had more problems with vices such as smoking, alcohol and overeating, and more often said and did things they regretted later.

Of course, consistently running behind doesn't necessarily classify you as being thoroughly without discipline. It's a funny thing. You might be a model of willpower in some areas of your life, yet completely lacking in others. Even successful, accomplished people lack self-control in certain areas. My seminars for the punctually challenged typically include successful lawyers, engineers and even a psychotherapist or two. Former President Bill Clinton is a prime example of an intelligent, hard-working, ambitious man who sometimes has difficulty with self-control. He initiated foreign policy, wrote legislation and ran the country, but couldn't get to a meeting on time.

Wanting it All

Why is it so difficult to exercise discipline? For some, it's simply about wanting it all. We want to sleep late, yet still eat French toast for breakfast, read the paper and stop at the dry cleaners before work.

Like the Peter Panners in Cure Two, some people balk at having to live by real-life limitations and make grown-up choices. Instead, they gravitate toward an "all things possible" mind-set, convincing themselves that they don't have to give anything up. Unfortunately, life doesn't always accommodate this type of thinking.

For most of us, accepting discomfort is difficult. Yet that's really what self-discipline and successful habit-breaking are all about—the ability to make sacrifices and to accept limitations. It's the strength to choose what's best in the long run instead of what feels good right now, even if it means having to give something up.

Why Do Some People Lack Self-Control?

Where did all this start? Are some people just born with more strength than others? Or is it something we learn over time? Of course, there is no single reason why one person has trouble resisting the urge to sleep late or to do one last thing before leaving the house. But there are a few ingredients that play a part in determining whether you'll be a model of control or an example of impulsiveness:

- Your experience with effort and discomfort
- Genetics
- Family influences

Experience with Effort and Discomfort

Social scientists have found that how much self-control a person has usually correlates with how much past experience they've had with self-control. Psychology researchers Robert Eisenberger and Michael Adornetto found that the more children were exposed to delayed rewards, the more self-control they demonstrated in later challenges. For instance, when parents insist that their child stick to his tuba practice schedule even though it might be boring and tedious, they teach the child to accept discomfort and to put forth effort toward a goal.

An interesting 1988 study by researchers Mischel, Shoda and Peake demonstrates how willpower habits really do carry over into adulthood. In this experiment, researchers studying self-control gave young children a piece of candy and asked each to sit alone in a room. The children were told they could eat the candy right away, but that if they could manage to hold off until the researchers came back, they would receive five more pieces. Years later, when the scientists followed up on the children, they found that those who exercised self-control by not eating the first piece of candy continued to demonstrate more self-control as adults. They also tended to be more successful in both their careers and personal lives.

Genetic Makeup

Another factor in the development of self-control is the functioning of the prefrontal cortex portion of the brain. Daniel

Amen, M.D., author of *Change Your Brain, Change Your Life*, describes the PFC, often termed the "executive control center," as being responsible for skills such as time management, impulse control and organization. "Our ability as a species to plan ahead and use time wisely is heavily influenced by this part of the brain. Without proper PFC function, it is difficult to act in consistent, thoughtful ways and impulses can take over," notes Dr. Amen.

Family Influences

Families wield a great influence when it comes to acquiring self-control. The primary part parents play is an important one—that of role models. Parents who practice restraint in their daily lives show children by example and their children come to see willpower as a normal part of life. In fact, many timely people I interviewed attributed their promptness to parents who stressed self-control and adherence to the "rules of society."

Families also influence the development of a child's behavior through love and affection. In his book, *The Impulsive Personality*, Howard Wishnie, M.D. explains that a child growing up without consistent amounts of each sometimes develops a sense of anxiety and deprivation. To soothe his anxieties, the child may develop an "I want everything now" attitude and have difficulty tolerating discomfort or frustration.

Of course, families aren't the only ones who influence your self-control and punctuality. Neurobiologist Irving Kupfermann of Columbia-Presbyterian Medical Center theorizes that our habits produce physical alterations in the neural pathways of our brains. When we perform an action repetitively or make the same decision repeatedly, our neural pathways strengthen in a particular direction and become like well-worn forest paths. Our tendency to follow those paths increases with every repetitive action we take. Habits are not established overnight, but are ingrained little by little, choice by choice.

Does Your Discipline Muscle Need Exercising?

Could your self-discipline use some improvement? Ask yourself the following questions:

- Do I have several bad habits that I've tried repeatedly, but unsuccessfully, to conquer?

- Do I tend to play things by ear, rather than sticking to a schedule?

- Do I frequently say or do things I regret?

- Do I have difficulty starting projects?

- Am I usually impatient when I have to wait?

- Do I lack long-range goals and daily plans?

If you answered yes to three or more of the above questions, you may be an "Indulger," a person for whom tardiness is rooted in low self-control. If this strikes a cord with you, you may benefit from the exercises in this chapter.

DEVELOPING DISCIPLINE

There are three important keys to building your willpower:

- Increase your tolerance for discomfort.

- Practice making transitions

- Become a planner and goal setter.

In the pages that follow, you'll learn not only how to increase your punctuality, but also to exercise more willpower in other aspects of your life. As you get in the habit of practicing these three steps, you'll most likely find that self-discipline isn't the onerous grind you may have envisioned, but rather an interesting way to challenge yourself and explore your inner strengths.

Increase Your Tolerance for Discomfort

Let's face it, most of us are born with the basic urge to do whatever is most comfortable; we're natural hedonists. Yet the ability to give up what you'd like to do in favor of what you should do is an important part of being on time. The following exercises will help you become accustomed to making those small sacrifices.

Exercise One

Each day for one week, give yourself experience with discomfort. Practice giving up something small, just for that day. If you normally drink two cups of coffee, drink one and a half. If you typically spend twenty minutes in the shower, spend just fifteen. Leave the house in the morning without doing something you normally feel you have to do. Think of it as a game, a test of your will against your whims.

If you experiment every day with "giving something up," you'll begin to build tolerance for discomfort. You'll also begin to realize that sacrificing small things is not as uncomfortable as you may have thought. It can, in fact, be quite freeing. Remember, willpower is like a muscle—the more you use it, the stronger it will get. Keep in mind these words by Edwin C. Bliss, author of *Doing It Now*:

> *"Just as you learn to walk by walking, or to juggle by juggling, you learn to exercise self-discipline by exercising self-discipline. But you don't just "will" yourself the ability to walk or to juggle—you take it one small, tentative step at a time, repeat those small steps until they become habitual and then take larger steps."*

When you find yourself procrastinating or giving in to the temptation to do one last thing before leaving the house or office, stop and remind yourself that sometimes it's necessary to give up feeling good now in order to feel good in the long run. Remember that with each discomfort comes more long-term self-control.

Exercise Two

Create a set of mantras. Just as mantras help Producers deal with the urge to do too much, they also help Indulgers exercise discipline. When you find yourself trying to squeeze in one last thing before you leave, use the wake-up signal you created in Cure Two and repeat the following mantra:

"Is this activity really necessary to get me where I'm going? Does it need to be done now, or even today?" Get in the habit of reminding yourself that whatever it is can probably wait.

Practice Making Transitions

How many times have you been in the midst of reading a newspaper, magazine or report, looked up at the time, and said, "I'd better get going," then thought, "...as soon as I get to a good stopping point"? You kept reading even though you knew it was time to stop, and ended up late.

It's ironic, isn't it? We procrastinate starting something, than once we do start, we procrastinate stopping. Part of the difficulty in stopping any activity midstream is simply the age-old struggle of pleasure versus pain that affects every one of us. Transitions are uncomfortable. Moving from one activity to another when we're perfectly happy and comfortable with what we're doing goes against our natural instinct for avoiding pain.

Interrupting a good thing can be especially difficult if you procrastinated starting to begin with. Whether you're cleaning the house or writing a report, it feels good to keep going until the project is finished. But the ability to muster the willpower not only to begin something when you should, but to quit when it's time is an important part of eliminating procrastination and lateness.

Exercise One

Practice making transitions with the following exercises:

- Repeat the mantra, "It won't get any easier in five minutes." When faced with something you really don't want to do but know you should—like getting out of bed in the morning—repeat this to yourself. This mantra works well because it's true; most difficult tasks don't get any easier when you put them off.

- When faced with a task that seems time-consuming or complex, such as preparing for a big presentation or reorganizing your closet, commit just five minutes to the activity. By allotting a short period of time, you take away the onerous element. Knowing you can stop soon will help motivate you to start. Once you put pen to paper or start opening drawers, chances are the laws of inertia will take over and you'll just keep going. Remember Newton's theory: "Things in rest tend to remain in rest. Things in motion tend to remain in motion."

- Practice stopping midstream. Whether you're in the middle of an engrossing novel or watching a good TV program, practice stopping before you're ready, if even for five minutes. Doing so will give you practice in making transitions so that when it really matters, you'll be up to the task.

Become a Goal Setter and a Planner

Winners focus, losers spray

—Edwin C. Bliss, author of *Doing It Now*

Even the most disciplined people use time-management techniques and tools to keep on track and to avoid the temptations of procrastination. A daily plan with time frames and priorities helps you to estimate how much you can accomplish in a day and encourages you to be realistic. When you have a written plan, you're less likely to drift off course.

Goals help to guide your activities and prevent you from getting so caught up in day-to-day events that you forget to focus on the important things in life. The most effective plans are based on long-term goals.

Those who lack plans and goals often find themselves drifting directionless through their days. Their energies become scattered and not really focused in any meaningful direction. Like hikers in the wilderness without a compass, they set out each day, trying this course and that and end up wandering around, off track and lost. It's only when they take the time to look ahead, to sit down and plan, that they achieve direction and progress.

Effective Goal Setting and Planning

- Do you make a plan for each day?
- Is your plan in writing?
- Do you include in your plan activities that will help you progress in your long-term goals?

If you answered "no" to any of the above questions, you may benefit from incorporating a few simple time management tools into your daily life.

Do you find yourself rebelling against the idea of a strict agenda? Perhaps you prefer to live spontaneously, to keep things flexible and to see how the day pans out. It's important to realize, however, that even the most simple plans, if done correctly, can actually result in more freedom and more time to spend on those things you enjoy.

Exercise One

Start by setting personal goals for both the long-term (three to five years) and the short-term (one year or less). Break your goals into the measurable steps you'll need to take to achieve them. Be sure to put your goals in writing and keep them posted in a place where you can see and think about them every day. While you're considering your goals, think about why they're important to you.

The following is an example:

Gwen, a retail store manager used to start each day by preparing her daily to-do list, instinctively packing it tightly with the usual activities—client calls, grocery shopping, working out at the gym and so on. She automatically based her plan on getting as much done as possible. Now when Gwen starts her to-do list, she keeps in mind one of her long-range goals—to win a promotion. To increase her chances, she's decided to be more timely, both in terms of arriving at work and in completing projects. She knows that if she schedules too tightly, she'll likely sabotage that goal. So Gwen prepares her to-do list with her goals in mind and schedules ample time between meetings.

Exercise Two

Create a daily plan based on your goals. "But I already have a to-do list," you might insist. The problem for many people is that their to-do lists are not well thought-out or realistic plans, but rather a random list of activities without time frames, priorities or a connection with long-range goals. Let's look at an example of a to-do list gone wrong. The following is a typical list that Bill, the software sales manager, put together each day.

- Prepare and submit proposal to Kline & Co.
- Write sales reports.
- Meeting with Mary Jones—discuss renewing contract.
- Call Tom Smith to discuss realignment of sales territory.
- Prepare for Abbott presentation.
- 3 o'clock sales presentation at Abbott Company
- Call Jane Doe at XYZ Corp. to discuss proposal.
- Pick up dry cleaning.
- Go to gym.
- Buy Mother's Day present.

- Go to post office to mail present.
- Chamber of Commerce meeting at 7:00 p.m.

Most mornings, Bill started his list feeling optimistic and energetic. He would ambitiously write down everything he wanted to accomplish, but would miss the boat in three important ways:

1. He didn't assign priorities to tasks.

2. He failed to give each activity a specific time estimate.

3. Because he didn't have time estimates and priorities associated with each task, Bill often overestimated what could be accomplished, put too much on his list and tackled the wrong things first. For example, he'd typically start working on an easy, low priority task such as sales reports before preparing for presentations. As meeting times drew nearer, Bill would realize he hadn't allotted enough time for preparation, and end up in a last minute scramble to make it on time.

On the other hand, if Bill itemized his activities in order of importance, he would find it easier to tackle the most difficult tasks first. Indeed, one of the primary principles of effective time management is to take on the most important or difficult tasks first thing in the morning when you're fresh and energetic. You can then concentrate on busy work toward the end of the day when you're less motivated and don't have quite as much energy.

Start each day by listing the activities you'd like to accomplish. Next, estimate how long each activity will take, and create a schedule by listing the most important tasks first. Here's an example of how Bill could have better scheduled his day.

8:15–9:15   Coffee & check & return e-mail/phone
              messages

9:15–10:15   Prepare for Abbott presentation.

10:15–11:00	Coffee/free-time
11:00–11:45	Prepare and submit proposal to Kline & Co.
11:45–12:45	Noon lunch meeting with Mary Jones—discuss renewing contract.
12:45–1:45	Buy Mother's Day present and go to the post office.
1:45–2:45	Call Jane Doe at XYZ Corp. to discuss proposal.
2:45–4:45	Abbott presentation
4:45–5:45	Write and submit sales reports
5:45–6:00	Pick up dry cleaning
6:00–7:00	Go to gym & grab a sandwich
Tomorrow:	Call Tom Smith - discuss realignment of sales territory.

When Bill prepares his schedule in priority order with time frames attached, he can easily see where he may run short of time. He can then decide which items, if any, should be moved to the next day.

Remember to put your list in writing. Doing so keeps your priorities front and center and helps you to stay mentally committed to the course.

Exercise Three

Adopt the policy: "Prepare, prepare, prepare":

- Call the day before to confirm any appointments you have.

- Obtain addresses, phone numbers and directions and put them with the rest of your things.

- When you have a meeting to attend, prepare everything you'll need in advance. Make sure you have a pen and pad of paper, laptop, pamphlets, brochures and anything else necessary.

Embrace the mantra, "check and double check." I'll never forget an incident that occurred as I was conducting research for this book. I was scheduled to administer a series of questionnaires to university psychology students on a Monday at 11 a.m. Having recently overcome my own tardiness problem, I proudly arrived outside the classroom fifteen minutes early. Not wanting to interrupt the class, I waited until 10:57 before opening the door. To my amazement, the room was empty. I ran frantically to the psychology office to find out where the class had gone. As it turned out, I had the wrong classroom and the right one was all the way across campus. Racing through buildings and down hallways, I finally made it ten minutes late to administer—ironically—a punctuality questionnaire.

The lesson here is to double check your facts—dates, times, locations, traffic conditions and anything else that has the potential for misinterpretation.

Exercise Four

For the next thirty days, practice sticking to your schedules. Late people are notorious for diverging from the chosen path, so be prepared for temptations. Understand that acquiring the habit of timeliness is like learning to play the piano. You won't be successful if you only practice once a week. To be a natural, you'll need to practice on a consistent basis. To establish new habits, you must weaken the old neural pathways and create and strengthen new ones.

Exercise Five

Enlist a buddy. Imagine how nice it would be to have someone in your life who acted as a partner to help motivate and cheer you on. In the working world our managers often serve this function. But in our personal lives, most of us tackle our goals and problems alone.

Find a friend, relative or associate who is also working toward a goal and join forces to motivate and inspire each other. Set both short- and long-term goals and meet regularly in person or over the phone. You'll find that having someone with whom to brainstorm and share ideas will be invaluable.

Learning to exercise self-control is one of the most fundamental skills you'll ever acquire. It's not only a necessary ingredient to help you get out the door on time, but it's also a factor that will help you in dozens of other areas of your life. As Daniel Goleman, in his best-selling book *Emotional Intelligence*, advises:

"Self-control, delaying gratification and stifling impulsiveness underlies accomplishment of any sort. People with this skill tend to be more highly productive and effective in whatever they undertake."

As you practice the tips in this chapter, you'll most likely notice an increase in willpower right away. Then just as you think you have got it mastered, you may experience a setback. Don't be discouraged. When you're used to instant gratification, gain with no pain, it can take a while to build consistent self-control. Anyone can increase their willpower. It just takes practice and the willingness to make a strong commitment to your goals.

REVIEW

- Self-control is the willingness to make sacrifices and accept that you can't have it all. It's giving up the extra cup of coffee, putting down the newspaper or doing whatever else it takes to get out the door on time.

- The level of self-control an individual has is usually determined by physiological and environmental factors and by past experience with effort and discomfort.

- Increase your tolerance for discomfort by giving up small things you normally feel you have to do.
- To allow new habits to strengthen and take root, be consistent with your punctuality.
- Practice making and adhering to a consistent schedule that includes time estimates and priorities.
- Enlist a goal partner with whom to share ideas and motivation.

CURE FIVE

Get Focused
and Organized

"We're behind you all the way."

—Motto of the Pennsylvania-based
Procrastinators Club of America,
an organization with 14,000 members.
It's estimated that there are millions
of would-be members who just
haven't gotten around to joining.

*"Last month I had an important client meeting in Boston," says
Russell, the vice president of research and development for a large
California technology company. "Since it was an early morning
appointment, I flew in the night before. But as I departed the plane, I
realized I'd forgotten the name of the company I was scheduled to visit.
It was too late to call my office on the West Coast and the meeting was
scheduled too early to call the next morning. I searched for a clue to the
name of the company, even dumped out my briefcase in the departure*

lounge, but came up with nothing. So I did a web search for engineering companies, hoping something would ring a bell. Struck out there too. When I got to the hotel, I frantically began calling—my wife, my associates—anyone I could think of who might be able to help me figure out who I was supposed to visit. Shortly after 8 a.m. the next morning, I received a call—the client wondering where I was. I stumbled out an excuse and rushed over, half hour late."

Russell falls into the category I refer to as the absent-minded professor syndrome. Absent-minded professors are perennially preoccupied folks who, while often intelligent and hard working, seem a little less focused and more distractible than the average person. They're not dim bulbs—quite the contrary. Professor types are typically very bright people who are simply less attentive to their surroundings and not particularly aware of other people. Because they're often caught up in their own worlds, these folks have a tough time with details, such as where they're supposed to be and when. Adding to the confusion is their tendency to lose things—essentials such as car keys, cell phones, purses, laptops, eyeglasses and shoes.

Do you fit into the absent-minded professor category? To find out, ask yourself the following questions:

- Do I frequently lose things such as car keys, jackets, credit cards or important documents?
- Do I often forget appointments, names and details of conversations?
- Have I frequently been accused of being inobservant or of not paying attention?
- Do I notice that the light has turned green only after the driver behind me honks?

- Do I regularly digress from the subject when speaking?

- Do I jump from one activity to another before the first is finished?

If you answered yes to two or more of these questions, this chapter is for you. To see where you fit into the picture, read through the three descriptions listed below. Most absent-minded professors match up with one or more and pinpointing your particular challenges is the first step in becoming more focused.

- Distractibility—Jumping from one task or activity to another before the first is finished; letting your mind wander.

- Forgetfulness—Forgetting appointments, losing car keys, cell phones, laptops or other personal items.

- Lack of awareness of others—Neglecting to notice what's going on in the world around you or failing to be observant of other people.

In the following pages, you'll learn how distractibility, forgetfulness, and inattention can affect your time management and what you can do about it. I'll discuss how you can overcome lateness by increasing your focus, becoming more observant and improving your organizational skills.

Distractibility

When we talk about distractibility, what we're really talking about is attention. The ability to focus attention varies tremendously from one person to the next and scientists have discovered that the level of a person's focus is pretty well established in childhood. How does this affect your timeliness? When you have a goal–getting to a meeting on time, for example—the ability to achieve that goal is directly linked to your ability to stay focused on it. Those who have difficulty getting from point A to point B without becoming sidetracked by points C, D, and E are people who will have problems arriving on time.

My friend Kathryn is a good example of a typical absent-minded professor. She'll be two blocks from her office when she'll see something in a store window—a donut, magazine or necklace—and stray off track just long enough to cause her to be late. She's a little like a Mexican jumping bean. Instead of moving forward, she bounces from one thing to another and has difficulty maintaining a straight course toward a destination.

Forgetfulness and Disorganization

"I love Russell dearly," explains his wife, Susanna. *"He's the best husband and father I could hope for. But sometimes it seems as if he's in his own little world, as though he's not really paying attention to what's going on around him. The other day, it was his turn to pick up the kids at school, but he forgot. Three months ago he overlooked the phone bill and our service was turned off. And getting him out the door is a particular feat—he's like one of the kids. Before we were married, I was never late. Now it's the story of my life. Russell's a wonderful man—kind, compassionate and very intelligent. I know he doesn't do these things on purpose and he seems sincerely surprised when I get angry with him. I think he's just caught up in his own world. His family tells me he's always been this way."*

Another common contributor to lateness is forgetfulness and the tendency to misplace items. People like Russell always seem to be missing something, whether it's a briefcase, a coat or one of the kids. Now, remember, Russell is a very bright man. His elementary school years were spent in special classes for gifted children and he's now a high-ranking executive. Forgetfulness rarely has to do with intellect, but more often with a kind of predisposition toward inattentiveness.

Preparing for an important meeting or a large dinner party can cause anyone to become preoccupied and scattered. Aren't we all more forgetful when we're very busy or under stress? But the absent-minded professor tends to be forgetful even under the best circumstances. He can look back on his life and see a pattern that is consistent regardless of the situation.

While forgetfulness and absent-mindedness can be more nature than nurture, there are ways you can improve upon the cards you were dealt. Later in this chapter, you'll learn how to improve your timeliness by increasing the levels of structure and organization in your life. But first, let's look at one more dimension of the absent-minded professor—lack of awareness of those around you.

Lack of Awareness of Others

When you took the quiz in the beginning of this chapter, how did you respond to the question, "Have you frequently been accused of being inobservant or not paying attention?" If you answered, "yes," it may be because your attention is often directed inwardly.

Inwardly-directed people tend to get caught up in their own introspection. Instead of focusing on the feelings or expectations of the person they're meeting, they tend to concentrate on what's going on in their own heads. Rather than focusing on "getting there," they're thinking about yesterday's presentation, tomorrow's social event or whether to attend a quantum mechanics seminar. While we all get caught up in what's going on in our own minds from time to time, absent-minded professors engage in the habit on a regular basis.

Most absent-minded professors don't intentionally cause aggravation and annoyance to those around them, and they rarely realize how harmful lateness is to their relationships. They're puzzled when people say to them, "You just don't value my time," because valuing someone's time is not something they're necessarily thinking about. This may seem self-absorbed or egotistical, but in reality, it's simply preoccupation and an unawareness of others.

Attention Deficit Disorder

Now let's look at an extreme case of the inability to stay focused. Psychologists have identified a syndrome called attention deficit disorder (ADD), which is described, in part, as "difficulty focusing on one task, disorganization, impulsivity, and forgetfulness." People with ADD tend to have trouble staying on course, completing projects and following through on ideas. A person who has a great deal of difficulty controlling his attention might also be diagnosed with ADD. Because of their tendency to be easily distracted, chronic lateness and procrastination are very common in ADDers.

In his book, *Change Your Brain, Change Your Life*, Dr. Daniel Amen, M.D. describes the distractions ADDers face as not necessarily external distractions as much as internal. "In class, during meetings or while listening to a partner, the person with ADD tends to think about unrelated things and has trouble staying focused on the issue at hand," notes Dr. Amen. Like the stereotypical inventor, they're constantly preoccupied by the thoughts in their heads—new ideas, inventions or creative concepts.

ADD can vary from mild to severe. At the mild end of the scale is what most of us think of as simple absent-mindedness, while those at the high end tend to have difficulty keeping jobs and functioning in everyday life.

For illustrative purposes, let's look further at ADD. Most scientific research on the subject suggests that it's an inherited biological condition in which the prefrontal cortex of the brain does not function normally. As you saw in Cure Four, the PFC is that small part of the brain that is thought to be responsible for controlling our impulses. Interestingly, patients with head injuries in which the prefrontal cortex is damaged often show symptoms similar to ADD, including distraction, disorganization and impulsiveness.

"Often, people with ADD can pay attention just fine to things that are new, novel, highly stimulating, interesting or frightening," explains Dr. Amen. "These things provide enough interest and stimulation that they activate the PFC so the person can focus and concentrate." Yet it's harder for people with ADD to consistently maintain mental focus in life's everyday activities.

Before you make the assumption that you have ADD, be aware that some psychologists believe this syndrome to be so over-diagnosed that it's lost much of its meaning. Certainly, everyone has a few symptoms—we are all disorganized, inattentive or impulsive to some extent—yet we don't all have ADD. If you really believe your symptoms to be severe enough to suggest ADD, however, seek the help of a well-trained professional.

If the absent-minded professor syndrome seems all too familiar, take heart, there is a light at the end of the tunnel. You're not necessarily doomed to being a distracted, disorganized person forever. Many ADD symptoms can be improved upon with simple techniques.

OVERCOMING THE ABSENT-MINDED PROFESSOR SYNDROME

In the following pages, you'll find exercises to help you increase your ability to stay focused and attentive and to raise your awareness of other people. There are three primary steps:

- Learn to stay focused on one thing for a sustained period of time
- Add structure and organization to your life.
- Increase your awareness and observation of other people.

Start by identifying your problem areas. Consider the three main characteristics of the absent-minded professor syndrome—distractibility, forgetfulness and a lack of awareness of others—and choose one particular area upon which you'd like to improve, one that most affects your life.

Learning to Stay Focused

As you've seen, absent-minded professors have difficulty getting from point A to point B without being sidetracked by points C, D and E. The following exercises are geared toward helping you maintain a straight path on the road you started down.

Exercise One

For one week, become aware of the occasions in which you become distracted, particularly those times when you're pulled off track from your destination. Be on the lookout for the instances when your mind wanders or when you leave one project before completing it to start another.

Exercise Two

Practice keeping your attention focused on a single act at a time. For instance, if your mind wanders when engaged in conversation, make it a point to pull yourself back on track. When you find yourself digressing from a point you are making, pause, take a deep breath, compose your thoughts and allow your mind to find its focus.

Using your watch or a clock, see how long you can keep your attention from being pulled away from the subject at hand and gradually try to increase that time.

Exercise Three

There are many ways to increase your mental focus, but perhaps the most effective is meditation. Many people associate meditation with relaxation, and to some extent, this is an accurate perception. It is, however, also a type of mental exercise. Just as physical exercise accomplishes more than one goal by improving both your body and state of mind, meditation not only relaxes you, but also increases your focus and awareness.

There are many types of meditations. The particular type you'll learn here is called mindfulness meditation. The purpose of this type of meditation is to direct your mind to one thing without becoming distracted. You learn to do this primarily by focusing on one thing—your breath—for increasing periods of time. When you attempt to focus on your breath, thoughts and emotions will interrupt your attention. Meditation teaches you to pull your attention back to your breath. To learn how you can incorporate simple meditation routines into your daily life, please turn to Appendix B.

Getting Structured and Organized

Adding structure and organization to your life is another effective key to overcoming the absent-minded professor syndrome. Absent-minded professors tend to keep things vague and flexible. Yet a day without structure is dangerous for this type of late person. Without a regular schedule, professors are more likely to get pulled off-track.

For people who tend toward forgetfulness and inattention, structure can also provide a kind of safety net—a way of arranging your life so that people and things are not forgotten.

Exercise One

Add structure to your life by using a phone app, electronic or print planner and making regular time slots for activities. Be as specific as possible. For instance, don't simply plan to work out three days a week. Instead, choose a precise day and time that you'll go to the gym. Louise, for example, shops for groceries on Monday evenings, goes to the gym on Tuesdays and Thursdays and pays bills and does her laundry on Saturday mornings. As much as possible, adhere to your chosen schedule.

Each Monday morning, look through your commitments for the coming week. If you are driving somewhere you haven't been before, this is the time to look up directions. Write down the telephone number and address and put it in your phone, briefcase or purse. Once each week, call to confirm appointments.

Exercise Two

Each morning, make a list of the items you would like to accomplish that day. Prioritize the entries either by listing them in priority order or by using a 1-2-3 or A-B-C approach. Assign realistic time frames for each activity and always start with the highest priority items first while you're fresh and clear-headed.

Next, create a short paragraph or list at the bottom of your daily plan for your long-term goals. This section is important because it provides a continual reminder of your hopes and dreams.

Record all your appointments, meetings and social engagements in your planner and review them frequently throughout the day. Be sure to carry over any undone tasks or unfinished business to the next day. After a month of following this exercise, you'll find that incorporating structure into your life will seem natural.

Please review Cure Four for an example of how to create realistic short- and long-term plans.

Exercise Three

Develop a system for staying organized. The following tips will help prevent you from losing things and forgetting appointments and will also increase your ability to operate efficiently:

- Have a specific place for everything. Always keep essentials, such as keys, briefcase, laptops, eyeglasses, purses and wallets in the same place. There's nothing more frustrating than being late because you couldn't find your keys.

- Organize your house and office so that things are separate and easy to find. Many department stores carry drawer separators and storage containers with individual compartments for keeping things neat and orderly. Store infrequently used items away so they don't clutter the objects you use often.

- Set up efficient filing systems for your computer and your printed items, then file items immediately. Keep a separate "pending" file for things that you'll need to review or handle in the near future.

- Try going "paperless." Use phone and computer applications for calendar appointments and activities, to jot down ideas and reminders and to store important documents. Don't work off scraps or loose pieces of paper, which have a tendency to get lost or misplaced. You'll find it much easier to perform a computer search for a needed item then to search through a stack of papers. In addition, electronic documents and appointments are easier to access from various locations.

- Be sure to back up your computer, phone or organizer on a weekly or more frequent basis. There are many resources for backing up your files, contacts and other important items, including cloud computing, Internet storage companies or external devices such as hard drives, CDs or flash drives. After you've finished backing up, be sure to test a few files to confirm that your backup was successful.

- The night before an appointment or meeting, put everything you'll need, such as your briefcase, portfolio, books, laptop or overnight bag, by the door so you won't need to rush around at the last minute looking for items.

- Always keep spares of frequently used items, such as car and house keys, hair dryers, nylons, shampoo, soap and makeup.

- Keep a clock in every room and a waterproof one in the shower. Professors tend to lose track of time and having reminders everywhere you look can help alleviate that problem.

Increasing Your Awareness of Other People

Attentiveness applies not only to staying focused on the task at hand, but also to having a certain amount of awareness of other people. As you've seen, absent-minded professors often have an inward focus. One way to overcome chronic tardiness is to change that inward orientation to an outward one. You'll find it much easier to be on time when your attention is focused on the person you're meeting rather than on yourself.

Exercise One

Become a good listener. Listen to others as though you'll be quizzed on it later. Pay attention to the sound of their voices, their facial expressions and their body language. Ask questions about their lives, their families, work and hobbies. Don't interrupt while people are speaking and try not to anxiously await your own turn to talk. Look each person in the eye and focus on what they are saying. Remind yourself to think outwardly, rather than inwardly.

As you complete the exercises in this chapter, you'll find that your focus, attention and awareness of other people will increase and your distractibility will decrease. Because you'll be able get from point A to point B without having your attention pulled away from the road you started down, your tendency to be late will diminish. You'll be more organized, less forgetful and more sensitive to the needs of others.

REVIEW

- Absent-minded professors are those whose lateness is due to a lack of focus and attention.
- Start by identifying your problem areas—distractibility, forgetfulness or a lack of attention.
- Begin to pay attention to the times you become distracted or are pulled off track, especially those times when distractions make you late.
- Practice sustaining your attention on a single activity or conversation for an extended period of time.
- Learn how to meditate as a way of increasing your focus and attention.

- Add structure and organization to your life by adhering to a set daily schedule and by getting organized in your home, office and life.
- Become more mindful of the people around you by practicing your observation and listening skills.

CURE SIX

Play by the Rules

"I came to the conclusion years ago that I would never be cool. I mean, really cool. The reason was that no matter how hard I tried, I was always on time."

—Craig Wilson, Columnist for USA Today

Brent is a well-known plastic surgeon in New York City. He's redraped the faces and resculpted the bodies of some of the most famous actresses and models in the world. But if you want an appointment with him, you'd better be prepared to wait because he's always booked months in advance. Once you are admitted into the sacred confines of his office, you'll have to cool your heels even longer because he always over-schedules. People wait for him, never the other way around. Brent admits he gets a kick out of this. As he strides through his plush waiting room, glancing down at the handful of prominent people waiting patiently, he feels important. Brent gains a sense of power and control from knowing that these people are willing to temporarily put their lives on hold for him.

Control—the feeling that we're in charge, important. Everyone likes being in control to some extent. But for some, the need to feel powerful or special is particularly compelling and can overrule their consideration of others. Chronically late people in this category typically have one or more of the following underlying motivations:

- The desire to feel powerful
- Difficulty accepting authority
- The need to feel special or unique

All three types of people are what I call "Rebels"—those who feel the need to regularly defy the rules. Interestingly, most rebels share three common characteristics:

- Unlike those in other tardy categories, rebels often feel little remorse. "I sort of get a charge out of keeping people waiting," says Dan, an author. "All of my past girlfriends have gotten angry, but it didn't really faze me. I kind of enjoyed it."
- Secondly, more men than women seem to populate this category. As one latecomer says, "It's a guy thing. You feel like you've got something over the next person if you can keep them waiting."
- Third, this type of late person seems to have the ability to control their lateness more so than other tardy types. Many report, for example, that they have no problem being on time to places or events that really matter to them, such as work, airline flights and interviews.

In the pages to come, I'll discuss each type of rebel, help you to determine which group you fall into and review what you can do to improve your time management.

Power Players

Power Players enjoy breaking the little everyday rules that most people take for granted. Doing so gives them a feeling of control and a temporary ego boost. When they do things their way, in their own time, power players feel in charge and important. In effect, they're saying, "I'm in command here. I run my own schedule."

Ironically, the need to assert power in this way often stems from feelings of powerlessness in a person's life. The power player frequently has lower than average self-esteem and seeks to control situations as a way of asserting the authority or superiority he'd like to have. For the person who feels uncertain or lacks confidence, the knowledge that other people are willing to wait helps bolster his sense of importance. The idea of rushing to arrive early and having to wait, on the other hand, prompts feelings of insignificance.

Authority Resistors

Rick, an intelligent, 38-year-old man, works as a lender for a financial institution. He currently makes considerably less money than he did in his last position as a trader for a Wall Street firm, where he was fired for continually failing to come to work on time. Although Rick was expected to be at his desk at 6:30 a.m. when the stock market opened, day after day he'd come strolling in twenty minutes late. One morning when Rick showed up late on a particularly volatile trading day, his manager walked up to him and screamed, "You're out!"

Rick's background has a lot to do with his tardiness. His father, a famous photographer and renowned perfectionist, was a strict authoritarian who made all family decisions with little input or consultation from the other members. Whether it was the shirt Rick wore or the way he answered the phone, his father always saw room for improvement. Rick felt as though he had little control over how he lived his life and as if every decision was second-guessed, every action met with criticism.

Rick's real troubles began about six months after he landed his position. He gradually began to resent anyone, however well intentioned, giving him advice or reminding him of company policy. When his manager began insisting that Rick come in early to cover the trading desk before the market opened, he began a slow burn. No matter how angry his manager got, Rick stubbornly refused to give in and arrive on time.

When he lost his job, Rick was surprised at how difficult it was to secure a comparable position at the same salary. Now that he pulls in a much lower paycheck, he has second thoughts about the old job, yet continues to insist that the working environment was intolerable. "I'd like to get my old job back, but I can't stand having someone breathing down my neck," Rick says.

Rick's wife, Carol says their marriage is a happy one, as long as she doesn't give even the appearance of control. "We get along great," Carol says. "But he seems to resist even the most innocuous suggestions. I rarely make recommendations to Rick anymore because he has a way of digging in his heels at even the slightest hint of control."

If Rick's story sounds familiar, you may be the type of late person who practices little daily acts of defiance. You may not even be completely aware of the times you defy and your actions may be so habitual and long-standing that defying is second nature.

For authority resisters like Rick, the normal compromises and adjustments of life take on larger-than-life dimensions. He sees even the most common expectations as unreasonable demands. Sometimes he even resists doing something merely because someone else expects him to do it. When Rick thinks he's being too accommodating, he feels weak and compliant. But what he sees as "too accommodating" often just meets the normal standards of cooperation.

Resentment

Authority resistors are often people who harbor resentment. In the case of an employee, it might be some aspect of his job, such as the boss, salary, responsibilities or policies of the company for which he works. If he feels helpless to do anything constructive about his situation, he may opt for what's called "passive-resistance," a way of outwardly appearing to comply, while inwardly resisting. He may agree, for example, to show up to work on time but repeatedly fail to live up to that commitment.

Authority resistors often dislike open confrontation, preferring instead to resist subtly by simply not doing whatever it is that's expected of them. Because they don't openly defy, other people often don't realize the extent to which the authority resistor is rebelling. So it can be confusing to those near him when he habitually fails to live up to the things he says he's going to do.

How does this type of resistance get started in the first place? As you saw with Rick, sometimes authority resisters are those who have been raised in a particularly controlling environment. Other people, however, simply have difficulty constructively expressing their feelings and finding practical solutions to their problems. They resort to expressing their unhappiness and frustration with lateness, procrastination and absenteeism. Ironically, rebel employees are often so busy defying, they fail to remember that they chose to take the job and agreed to certain company guidelines, such as arriving on time.

Special Seekers

More subtle than the power player or the authority resistor is the special seeker. These are people who have an inordinate desire to break free from the crowd. Flouting the rules of society assures them that they're different. It's a way of saying, "I march to my own drummer." While power players and authority resistors often act purposefully, special seekers are typically unaware of the motives behind their actions.

The special seeker is the category in which you'll find a number of artists, musicians and actors. These rebels yearn to stand apart from "ordinary" folk, to distinguish their lives from what they, consciously or not, think of as the average person's mediocre, conventional life. They pride themselves on being nonconformists and often have a sense that they are different than the average Jane or Joe.

Although, intellectually, special seekers know that certain rules have a place in society, the notion of complying with those rules makes them feel stifled and less individualistic. Here is an example of one woman's quest to feel unique:

Nikki, a forty-year-old former art student has, for the past three years, worked part-time as a dental assistant. Nikki's scheduled start time at the office is 8:30 a.m., yet unfailingly, she comes dashing in around 8:50. The doctor for whom she works has tried everything he can to get her to come to work on time. "Nikki is supposed to arrive thirty minutes before the office opens to unlock the doors, get out the patient charts, and check the answering service for messages," says the doctor. "But twice last week I had to act as my own receptionist because my first patient arrived before Nikki."

Like many tardy people, Nikki is a dichotomy. Impeccably attired and well-spoken, she presents the image of an efficient employee. Yet underneath her well-presented exterior is a woman who is insecure in her individuality. The idea of marching down the sidewalk at exactly 7:40 along with the rest of the commuters makes her feel like just a working drone. She loathes the idea of being part of the crowd, and because she's unsure of her own uniqueness, these images have a greater-than-average distaste. By stalling and rushing, she does things just a little differently. Nikki wants to be a model employee, but she can never quite overcome the habit of marching to her own drum.

For people like Nikki, the idea of following the rules is simply too ordinary and being ordinary carries with it the stigma of having failed to achieve her fantasy life—a life brimming with interesting, exciting activities and successes. By marching to her own clock, she finds an effective, if short-lived, way of feeling special.

Of course, being a rebel is not necessarily an undesirable trait. Many of the most talented, accomplished people in history have made a point of breaking the rules. There is, however, a difference between breaking the rules to express your creativity and breaking the rules out of insecurity or a need to assert control. There are many constructive ways to be unique or to express your individuality without undermining your own happiness or inconveniencing those around you. In the next section you'll learn how to find your own inner power and uniqueness and how to stop looking for control in all the wrong places.

OVERCOMING THE REBEL HABIT

There are three steps to managing the rebel habit:

- Become aware of when and why you rebel
- Learn that cooperation is a part of everyday life
- Find control and power in more constructive ways

Become Aware of When and Why You Rebel

Rebels are often unaware of their own resistance habits, so they end up resisting everything from the benign, such as taking out the trash at night, to the serious, like showing up late for work every day. They don't necessarily choose their battles consciously, but rather habitually react to whatever is in front of them at the time. The following exercises are intended, therefore, to increase your awareness of the ways you defy and why.

Exercise One

Begin to recognize when you rebel. Do you feel your hair rising when you think someone expects something from you? Do you find yourself defying rules or policies to which other people have no problem adjusting? Do you rebel against even benign expectations, such as paying bills or attending meetings on time? Can you see any patterns in your defiance? For example, do you resist rules primarily at work, or do you defy in your family life as well? For now, simply try to notice your patterns.

Exercise Two

Once you've recognized the occasions you resist, try to stop and ask yourself why you're choosing to defy the rules and what triggers your behavior. Get in the habit of asking yourself the following questions:

- Why am I defying this request or rule?
- Is this request or rule unreasonable?
- Is it necessary or practical?

Instead of automatically resisting rules and expectations, try to look at each situation individually, and ask yourself if defying really makes sense. You may see that it's easier and more practical for you to change your own behavior than to expect everyone else to alter theirs.

Exercise Three

When you're tempted to break the rules, ask yourself, "Did I freely commit to this?" Sometimes we forget that we've agreed to follow the rules, either implicitly—such as accepting a job offer, or explicitly—by saying, "I'll meet you at 8:00 p.m."

Remember that whether you resent it or not, if you've told someone you'll be somewhere at a specific time, you've made a promise that you should live up to.

Exercise Four

Get in the habit of asking yourself what will happen if you don't comply with a particular rule or request. Will it negatively impact another person's job or life? Will it inconvenience those around you? Try to look at the request from the other's point of view. Instead of digging in your heels, broach the issue openly and honestly.

Learn that Cooperation Is a Part of Everyday Life

Cooperation is an important part of life, yet rebels often perceive normal requests as unreasonable demands. It's important, therefore, to see other people's expectations and needs not as an infringement, but as a natural part of life. Because you may not be accustomed to giving up control to another person, it can be difficult to change your thinking. The following exercises are designed to help you get used to and enjoy the feeling of relinquishing control without feeling that you're compromising your own rights or individuality.

Exercise One

Practice periods of cooperation, times when you comply with another person's request or expectations when normally you would resist. If, for instance, you and your wife plan to go to the movies, let her choose what you'll see. Then go with an open mind and without resentment. During these cooperation exercises, pay attention to your own reactions and the reactions of others. You'll probably find that acquiescing is not nearly as bad as you thought it would be. You may even find giving up control to be a pleasant experience and be surprised at the positive responses you receive from the people around you.

Exercise Two

Start thinking of yourself as a team member. Instead of viewing life as "them versus me," imagine that your goals are linked with those around you. Try to act in ways that will benefit the entire team, not just you. For example, when your spouse asks you to be ready to leave for a restaurant at 7:30, instead of resenting that request, learn to view it as your contribution toward the mutual goal of having an enjoyable evening.

Exercise Three

Apologize when you are late. It's certainly reasonable to be late occasionally, but not consistently. So if you have to be late, don't hesitate to apologize. Many rebels believe that apologizing is equivalent to admitting weakness, but in reality it's exactly the opposite. To apologize sincerely, to take responsibility for your actions, is an indicator of strength.

Find Control in More Constructive Ways

Find other, more positive ways to feel unique and powerful in your life. Instead of attempting to gain control by resisting other people's rules or expectations, try finding ways to gain power and a sense of specialness within yourself so that you won't be tempted to acquire it through rebellion.

Exercise One

Learn to distinguish yourself in positive, constructive ways. Because rebels sometimes lack a strong sense of who they are, they subconsciously try to set themselves apart by breaking society's rules. Instead, try to distinguish yourself by finding your own sense of individuality.

You might, for example, find your passion in volunteerism or social work, in environmental causes or in political activism. Take some time to think of something that interests you and start exploring your options. Talk to people, join an organization or look on the Internet. You'll likely find dozens of ways to feel unique without having to resort to breaking the rules.

Exercise Two

Sign up for a course in assertiveness training or negotiating. These types of classes teach you how to constructively ask for what you need, rather than resorting to passive-aggressive methods. Assertiveness training can teach you how to gain true power by learning how to effectively compromise and openly negotiate for what you want.

Because the rebel habit typically has its roots in childhood, it can be a challenging one to break. However, if you pay attention to when and how you rebel, understand your motivations and practice periods of cooperation, you'll find changing a natural process.

REVIEW

- Chronic lateness can be the result of a need to feel powerful, a desire to resist authority or a drive to feel unique. This type of resistance can often be linked to underlying insecurities.
- Begin to pay attention to the occasions when you rebel and ask yourself why you're choosing to resist.
- Get in the habit of asking yourself if you freely committed to whatever's being expected of you.
- Practice cooperation periods when you comply with others when you would normally resist.
- Think of yourself as a team member sharing common goals with those around you.
- Find other ways to feel unique and powerful by pursuing a hobby or skill in which you have an interest.
- Sign up for assertiveness training or negotiating classes to learn to assert yourself constructively.

CURE SEVEN

Respect Yourself

"There is overwhelming evidence that the higher the level of self-esteem, the more likely one will treat others with respect, kindness and generosity."

—Nathaniel Brandon

In the world of psychology, the words "self-esteem," "anxiety" and "perfectionism" are often used in the same conversation because they are characteristics that tend to influence and effect each other. The first, self-esteem, has a profound effect on nearly every aspect of our lives. The way we feel about ourselves affects everything we think, say and do.

Just what is self-esteem, and what does it have to do with chronic lateness? First and foremost, self-esteem is respecting and liking yourself. It's feeling proud of who you are and the way in which you live your life. There are three primary ways in which self-esteem can affect punctuality:

- When you suffer from low self-esteem, you tend to expect

less of yourself. Because of those low expectations, you may set lower standards for the way in which you live your life. Chronic lateness, unreliability and procrastination can be part of those lower-than-normal standards.

- Low self-esteem can cause feelings of anxiety or depression, prompting you to engage in the "evader syndrome." This is the attempt to alleviate anxiety by engaging in avoidance and perfectionism and can take precedence over moving forward.

- Low self-esteem can cause you to engage in what is known as "self-handicapping."

As adults, many of us have grown into our skins and have come to like and respect ourselves. Yet sometimes old habits from not so secure pasts continue to dog us even after the original source has long been alleviated. In the pages to come, you'll learn how to get past the insecurities that may be affecting your life and how to overcome habits like procrastination, perfectionism and anxiety.

Expectations

Some people, the lucky ones, have an inner core of self-esteem that seems to carry them through life's ups and downs. They believe in themselves, and because of that belief, have high expectations for themselves. For most people, living up to their own expectations is instinctual—it's what is known as a self-fulfilling prophecy. Self-esteem, expectations and actions form a kind of circle in each of our lives. Self-esteem determines what kind of expectations we have of ourselves, those expectations influence our actions, and our actions, in turn, shape our levels of self-esteem.

Unfortunately, the self-fulfilling prophecy can also work to our detriment. When you lack a healthy sense of pride in yourself, your actions reflect those feelings. Showing up late for work or continually breaking commitments may be a way of living up to low expectations and may even seem natural.

Anxiety

When my friend, Victoria, gets ready for a party, she goes through a similar scenario each time. As she looks through her wardrobe, she starts to feel anxious. "I have nothing to wear," she worries. While she enjoys parties, Victoria never feels completely comfortable around new people and is afraid she'll be tongue-tied. Finding just the right outfit to wear gives her a measure of confidence and calms her fears to some extent.

As the time to leave nears, Victoria's anxiety increases. She tries on the outfit she had planned to wear, but is disappointed with her reflection in the mirror. Soon, she's trying dress after dress, hoping to find the perfect one. A pile of clothes begins to form on her bed and the time to leave passes, but Victoria continues frantically throwing on and stripping off clothes. By the time she's ready to leave, she's hopelessly late.

Anxiety is a common thread running through the lives of many late people. The urge to alleviate anxiety can be very strong, so much so that it can take precedence over our commitments. In Victoria's case, you saw how low self-esteem caused her to feel anxious, which, in turn, led to the pursuit of perfection as a way to relieve her fear. She instinctively tried to find a way to feel confident and concentrated her energies in one area that she could control—her appearance.

When Victoria finds the perfect dress for an occasion, it gives her a temporary sense that everything will work out, so finding the right clothes takes on an exaggerated importance. Instead of accepting her apprehension and moving in the direction she should go—the party—she focuses on the quick fix.

Certainly, perfectionism is not always a bad characteristic. Having high standards in life is important. However, when perfectionism is a response to anxiety, standards are often not only high, but unrealistic. When striving for perfection is motivated by fear, you can get caught in a counterproductive cycle of endlessly trying to alleviate an anxiety that won't go away.

The Evader Syndrome

Another way low self-esteem and anxiety can lead to chronic lateness is what I call the "evader syndrome." Instead of turning to perfectionism to relieve anxiety, the evader simply ignores the clock or finds other activities to help her avoid her commitments. She might begin puttering around the house fixing appliances or suddenly decide her jewelry needs polishing. Like an ostrich who buries its head in the sand, the evader has the ability to phase out the cause of her anxiety and concentrate instead on some menial task such as sharpening all the pencils in her office. It's only when she's down to the wire that the evader is finally able to force herself into action.

Some evaders are people who are prone to depression and have difficulty moving forward because of feelings of lethargy or hopelessness. These feelings can also cause anxiety as the individual feels guilt and remorse over their inability to manage tasks other people seem to take in stride. Leaving the house can seem like an insurmountable feat to a person who feels depressed.

Of course, everyone feels anxious from time to time, but most people still manage to get where they're going on time and avoid extreme procrastination. Why do some people respond to anxiety more strongly than others?

Research has shown that some people experience a kind of chronic anxiety. They feel anxiety more deeply and more frequently than others. What's more, they may not recognize why they're anxious or know how to move past their feelings. When you don't understand or recognize your feelings, you can get in the habit of responding to them automatically, instinctively doing things to feel better.

Anxiety and perfectionism are not the exclusive right of the late. In punctuality studies, however, late people were found to be more anxious overall than timely people, not only in circumstances such as job interviews or first dates, but also with life in general. Many seemed to live with a kind of long-term sense of unease.

Psychologists theorize that some people are simply born with more sensitive or apprehensive natures, which can predispose them to procrastinate in uncomfortable or intimidating situations.

Negative Self-Talk

If anxiety is making you late, you might be compounding the situation with negative self-talk. While Victoria gets ready for the party, she runs through a mental litany of all the things that might go wrong. "I'm so bad at making conversation with new people," she frets. "I can never find anything interesting to say." You can hardly blame Victoria for having a tough time pushing herself forward when she's anticipating failure. When you envision the worst that will happen, it's hard to leave your comfort zone and get motivated to go anywhere.

Most of us have an inner voice that lets us know when we've been rude, gotten out of line or misbehaved in some way. We chastise ourselves for saying the wrong thing at parties, for forgetting our parents' birthdays and for cheating on our diets. Unfortunately, for those with lower than average self-esteem, that small inner voice works overtime, exaggerating any tiny infraction and worrying endlessly over minor events.

Negative self-talk is usually so automatic and subconscious, we're unaware we're doing it. But it's a habit that over time takes root and gradually erodes our self-worth. We know that children and adults alike flourish when they're praised and complimented, yet we often forget to extend the same nicety to ourselves. Can you imagine working for a boss who berated you the way you sometimes berate yourself? And if our friends talked to us the way we talk to ourselves, we'd certainly send them packing. It's an unfortunate fact, however, that it's more natural to heap blame and criticism on ourselves than to compliment and reassure.

How It All Started

Edmund J. Bourne, Ph.D., author of *The Anxiety and Phobia*

Workbook, suggests that heredity is, to some extent, a contributor to both anxiety and low self-esteem. "What is inherited seems to be a general personality type that predisposes one to anxiety," notes Dr. Bourne. Other psychologists attribute family and environmental influences and our own repetitive actions to the development of self-esteem.

What is definitive is that self-esteem is something that, to a great extent, anyone can acquire. It's simply a way of thinking, acting and talking that conveys respect. You don't necessarily need to have the right parents or the right upbringing to build self-esteem. It's entirely possible to develop it later in life.

BUILDING SELF-ESTEEM

"It is never too late to be what you might have been."

—George Eliot

Of course, you can't simply wave a magic wand to gain greater self-worth. For some people, it's best undertaken with professional help. For others, however, practicing a few fundamental principles can make a real difference:

- Expect more from yourself.
- Tame your inner critic.
- Challenge yourself.
- Build and maintain friendships and family ties.

Expect More of Yourself

Our self-image and our habits tend to go together. Change one and you change another.

— Dr. Maxwell Maltz

One of the keys to gaining self-esteem is to start expecting more of yourself, to begin doing what's right, even when it's not easy. It means moving closer to what you consider to be the ideal you.

But isn't this putting the cart before the horse? Don't you first need years of therapy to increase your self-esteem, after which your actions will, in turn, improve? Not necessarily. Sometimes the best way to build self-esteem is to act as though you already have it.

There is an old adage: "To do is to be." When you behave like the person you want to be, you are that person for the moment. If you behave in that manner long enough, you become that person.

Exercise One

The first step in expecting more of yourself is to envision the type of person you'd like to be. Ask yourself how you want to live your life, what's important to you and what your values are. List three adjectives that describe your aspirations. For example, perhaps integrity is important. Write this down and elaborate—what does that mean to you? Does it mean keeping your word? Does it mean being considerate of others? Perhaps it means being someone upon whom others can count.

For the next month, practice living up to the standards you've identified. Reward yourself for even for the smallest attempt. Pat yourself on the back any time you follow your ideals.

Tame Your Inner Critic

I used to think, "I can't do this". Now I say "Let me try; maybe I can."

—Joan Lunden, former host, *Good Morning America*

As you saw earlier, many people with low self-esteem engage in negative self-talk. You may beat yourself up over things great and small, from your clothes to your career missteps and relationship set-backs. It's important to recognize the times you engage in negative self-talk and interrupt the process. Doing so is a critical part of building self-esteem.

Exercise One

One effective way of interrupting negative self-talk is to engage in a minute of silent meditation. Simply breathe deeply and focus on your outgoing breaths for one minute. Count four breaths and then start over again. This practice will help you suspend the chattering in your mind and gain control over your thoughts. For more on meditation techniques, see Appendix B.

Exercise Two

Next, replace the negative talk with positive talk. Jane Massengill, MFCC, a San Ramon, California personal coach calls this "throwing darts at your gremlins." Start by taking an objective look at what you say to yourself and question whether any negative statements are really accurate. Have a laugh as you notice the absurdity of some of your fears. Then use one or more of the following mantras to get back on track:

- "I'm fine just the way I am. I don't need to be perfect."
- "It's normal to have anxieties about this kind of thing."

When you catch yourself engaging in negative self-talk, remember the words of the late Richard Carlson in his best-selling book, *Don't Sweat The Small Stuff*:

"Remind yourself that it's your thinking that is negative, not your life ...It takes practice, but you can get to the point where you treat your negative thoughts in much the same way you would treat flies at a picnic: You shoo them away and get on with your day."

Another best-selling author, Jack Canfield, known for his *Chicken*

Soup for the Soul series, recommends, "Anytime you're scared and afraid to take action, repeat, 'Oh, what the heck, go for it anyway.'" It's normal to feel fear, but you can get past it. Even the seemingly most self-assured people have to push themselves past their fears.

I'll never forget a meeting I once attended in which former U.S. Secretary of State Warren Christopher was the speaker. An audience member asked him what he would have changed about his past actions or himself. Mr. Christopher answered that he wished he weren't so shy. This was an illuminating moment for me—to realize that even the most successful people in the world have insecurities and fears. They simply learn to move forward in spite of them.

Exercise Three

The next time you feel anxious, try to think of your feelings as those of excitement. The physiological tension you feel when you're anxious is very much like the feelings you have when you're excited. It's your perception of those feelings that make the difference. When you're preparing to go to a party, think of that twinge of anxiety as a ripple of excitement. Concentrate on how much you're looking forward to seeing the host's new house or how delicious the food will be. Focus on why this event will be fun, not on why it won't be.

Exercise Four

Let go of perfectionism. Every day for the next week practice leaving the house or office without making things perfect. You might leave the bed unmade or your desk in a mess. Notice how it feels to "chill out" and let things go. You'll probably find it liberating.

Challenging Yourself

"A ship is safe in port, but that's not where it's meant to be".

—Unknown

One of the best ways to deal with anxiety is to learn to push past fear. Learn how to face your fears and let go of any "fatal flaws" holding you back. Remember, feelings of fear are normal. It's what you do with those feelings that matters.

Exercise One

Do something that takes courage. Think of something you've always wanted to do but on which you've procrastinated because of fear. This can be something as simple as striking up a conversation with the person next to you on the train or as complex as learning to play the violin.

Take up rock climbing or sign up for gourmet cooking classes. Do whatever gets you out and away from your comfort zone. The more you push yourself with little acts of courage, the more you'll find you are capable of. Soon your fear will be something you accept as part of the human experience and you'll be able to move through it.

Exercise Two

Prior to taking on your challenge, run through a mental dress rehearsal. Picture yourself successfully carrying it out. For example, if you decide to take up golf, envision yourself at the golf course executing the perfect swing.

Now envision the worst that could happen. You completely miss the ball and fall to the ground in a heap. Imagine picking yourself up, having a good laugh and carrying on. Anticipate handling any faux pas with grace and humor.

Once you get used to seeing fear and failure not as deterrents but as necessary parts of a successful life, you'll become more comfortable with putting yourself "out there." You'll begin to see fear and anxiety as opportunities to prove to yourself that you are just as competent and capable as all those people you've been admiring.

Exercise Three

Do something you love. Sometimes anxiety and low self-esteem are rooted in a lack of purpose in life. People who feel that their lives have direction and meaning tend to feel happier, more satisfied and to have a greater sense of fulfillment.

Take at least one hour sometime in the next few weeks to sit down and ask yourself some important questions:

- What would I like to accomplish with my life? At the end, what would I like to look back on with pride and contentment?
- What do I most value in life—my family, career, material goods, friendship, spirituality?

Exercise Four

Now that you've thought about what's most important to you and what kinds of things would make you feel fulfilled, write down one item on which you might realistically start in the coming weeks.

If, for instance, your dream is to join a rock and roll band but have a family and children, sign up for guitar lessons. I have a colleague who enrolled in a local music school and after several years of lessons, was good enough to join a local group. During the day, he's an investment banker, but on weekends you'll find him performing with his rock band at local clubs.

Build and Maintain Friendships and Family Ties

Many of us are so caught up in our daily lives—working, raising kids, maintaining a household—that we neglect one of the strongest builders of self-esteem: our connections with friends and family. These are the people who build our self-esteem by giving us a sense of belonging and a reality check when we're too hard on ourselves. As Sam Horn, author of *Concrete Confidence* says:

"Many people think that getting together with friends is something you do when all your other obligations are taken care of... but by taking

the time to nourish yourself with friendships, you will like yourself and your life even more—the essence of confidence."

Exercise One

At least once each week, call someone dear to you, just to catch up. If they're local, make a date to get together for an hour. Don't merely rely on email, voicemail and text messages to stay in touch.

Increasing self-esteem and lessening anxiety are skills anyone can learn. As you work through the exercises in this chapter, your confidence will likely increase and you'll begin to experience less anxiety. The urge to get caught up in anxiety-reducing activities will be lessened and the perfectionism and evader habits that make you late won't be as relevant anymore.

REVIEW

- Low self-esteem, anxiety, depression and perfectionism are each contributors to chronic lateness.
- Begin to expect more of yourself—do what's right, even when it's not easy.
- Replace negative self-talk with praise.
- Let go of perfectionism.
- Challenge yourself by stepping out of your comfort zone and doing things you'd like to do but of which you are afraid.
- Build and maintain close connections with friends and family.

PART THREE

KEYS TO SUCCESS

A Few Words on Habit Changing

"For every complex problem, there is an easy answer, and it is wrong."

—H. L. Mencken

Before you set out to practice the strategies and exercises in this book, please take a moment to understand the basic psychology behind habit changing.

There are some common misperceptions surrounding what it takes to break a habit. Most of us think that if we simply polish up our resolve and try very hard, we'll stop doing whatever it is that's bothering us.

The scenario goes something like this: you start out strong, full of determination. Time management is given top priority and because you are so motivated, you make headway almost immediately. You're early to work for the first time in months. Your boss is ecstatic. "This isn't so difficult after all," you declare. Then human nature steps in. You relax your efforts, other activities distract you and pretty soon you've reverted to your old ways.

Look back on other habits you've tried to change. Chances are you weren't able to reform overnight. Each time you tried and failed, you probably gave up for a while, then went back to the drawing board.

SUCCESSFUL HABIT CHANGING

Changing any habit is difficult, especially a lifelong one. But the good news is that behavioral scientists have discovered what causes some people to succeed while others fail. They've found that certain methods work best and can be used across the board, whether you're trying to lose weight, stop smoking or quit nail biting. In the following pages, you'll learn how you can apply those techniques to lateness and procrastination and how best to ensure success. The three keys to successful habit changing are:

- Developing the right attitude
- Observing yourself
- Setting your goals and rewarding yourself

Developing the Right Attitude

"The greatest discovery of my generation is that human beings can alter their lives by altering their attitudes of mind."

—William James

As you put the lessons in this book into practice, remember that part of the process of overcoming lateness and procrastination is embracing and committing to a responsible, reliable way of life. Living in this way will not only increase your time management, but also build character and integrity. What's more, as you make reliability and courtesy a habit, you'll find that respect and consideration will come back to you.

Reliability and responsibility are based on the concept of putting other people's interests before or equal to your own. In his book, *Instant Analysis*, best-selling author and psychologist David Lieberman explains, "You cannot give a great deal of attention to yourself and to others simultaneously. If you're preoccupied with the 'I', there is little room left for the rest of the world."

Go Cold Turkey

Understand that to achieve success in your efforts, you must try to be reliable and on time for everything—your job, dinner parties, doctor appointments. It may feel like "no big deal" to be a few minutes late to work or five minutes late to meet friends, but for now, you must take the attitude that it is, in fact, critical to be on time. You must quit the lateness habit "cold turkey."

Bear in mind that bad habits are really nothing more than the wrong decision made over and over. Becoming punctual is a lot like kicking the habit of smoking. Researchers have found that smokers are more successful when they go cold turkey, when they've adopted the attitude that smoking is not an option. In this way, they don't have to decide each moment of every day whether or not to light up a cigarette. As each day passes without a cigarette, not smoking becomes the habit.

Don't Expect It to Be Easy

Everyone wants instant results. We all want to find that "guaranteed, simple secret" to success. But the truth is, there are no quick solutions for changing long-ingrained habits. As you saw in Chapter One, many habits—even negative ones—benefit us in some way. Consciously or not, they bring some type of pleasure, and pleasure can be tough to give up.

Back in 1954, two researchers named Olds and Milner found that pleasure could, in a sense, be addictive. They trained a group of rats to electronically stimulate their own medial forebrains, the area of the brain responsible for pleasurable sensations. When the animals pressed a metal bar, they received brain stimulation, which in turn caused enjoyable feelings. The desire for pleasure was so strong, the rats soon ignored food and drink in favor of the brain stimulation, eventually becoming dehydrated and emaciated.

While we humans may display greater self-control than these laboratory animals, we do have similar difficulties when attempting to kick habits that bring us some type of pleasure or benefit. So be prepared to make sacrifices and to try, fail and try again. This is perfectly normal.

Observe Yourself

By now you've probably noticed a recurring theme—the importance of taking a fresh look at your actions and your automatic behavior. Remember that automatic behaviors are all those little daily routines and habits we perform without thinking. While many automatic behaviors serve a purpose, they can make habit changing difficult. When we're not fully aware of our actions and our motivations, it can be hard to figure out how to change.

As you conduct your regular affairs over the next few months, remember to practice self-observation. Pay attention to the cues that bring about your late behavior. One of the purposes of observing yourself is to determine what your benefits are. Try to spot those benefits and understand their appeal.

Keep Track in Writing

Recording your patterns and progress in writing really does make a significant difference in the success of changing a habit. It not only helps you to see your behavior more clearly, but also strengthens your commitment toward your goal. Although this is one of the most important steps in habit changing, it's the one most people neglect.

Set Goals and Reward Yourself

The final component of successful habit changing is figuring out your goals and rewards. Do you want to be ten minutes early for work every day? Is it acceptable to arrive at parties fifteen minutes late? While you may be tempted to play things by ear, clear, written goals will help focus your efforts.

Decide too how you'll monitor yourself. You may want to schedule fifteen minutes a week to look at your progress and determine what went right or wrong. This is a good time to regroup and alter your strategy depending upon what worked for you and what didn't.

Rewards

Long ago, behavioral scientists discovered a simple concept called associative learning. To understand how associative learning works, let's look at the case of dog training. When you want a dog to perform a trick—"sit down," for instance—you ask the dog to sit, then you give him a treat. The likelihood that the dog will sit for you next time is directly related to what happened after he sat this time. If he was rewarded, he is more likely to sit again then if he received no reward.

Humans are similar in that our brains link actions with consequences. If we get something out of being late, be it stimulation or more time to sleep, our behavior is reinforced and we will continue to be late. If we get something out of being early, we'll associate earliness with rewards as well.

When you are trying to replace an old habit with a new one, rewards can act as potent motivators. Research has shown that people who are motivated with rewards are much more likely to improve then those who receive no rewards. Interestingly, negative reinforcements or punishments have not been found to be nearly as effective in habit changing.

Perhaps the most important aspect of rewards is that they be immediate. It is important to reward any progress, no matter how minor. When you acknowledge your small successes, you motivate yourself to do the same thing tomorrow, and the next day. So be sure to give yourself proper credit for any achievements you make.

How should you reward yourself? Of course, that depends on what motivates you. One woman I know allows herself a five-minute break each time she's successful. During those five minutes, she allows herself to do something totally frivolous and unproductive, such as reading a magazine or staring at the birds in the plaza below her office window.

Whatever you choose to do, even if it's just allowing a minute to smile and congratulate yourself, do it right away. You'll start linking pleasant feelings and actions with being on time, which will help move you even closer to your goal.

While immediate goals are effective, long-range goals can be especially motivating. You might negotiate with your spouse to buy something special if you achieve your goals. Or perhaps your manager might be persuaded to give you a day off when you've been early to work for two months in a row. In any case, try to set short-, intermediate- and long-term rewards for achievements you've made.

You're on Your Own:
A Final Note

I hope, in discovering the keys to effective time management, you've gained the tools and confidence to make progress with your goals. I hope that those same lessons will help you in other areas of your life as well. The intent of this book is not only to provide guidance in overcoming lateness, but also to assist you in developing organizational skills, lessening procrastination and increasing your ability to stay focused and on track.

At this point, you've likely developed insight into your own particular situation and heightened your awareness of the patterns and payoffs surrounding your lateness. You've chosen one or two lateness types that most closely resemble your own patterns and have selected three or four exercises that seem most appropriate for you. Your goals are in writing and you've come up with an action plan to move along the path to overcoming lateness and procrastination. Now you're ready to start practicing what you've learned.

Don't be afraid to ask for help if you need it. Sometimes all the written advice in the world can't replace a few good sessions with a psychologist, psychiatrist or personal coach. In my interviews and research, I've found that while psychologists and psychiatrists are best able to help deal with the deeper emotional issues such as low self-esteem or attention deficit disorder, personal coaches can be very effective in tackling the day-to-day behaviors that keep us in a rut. While coaching sessions often deal with emotional issues as well, the focus is on developing concrete steps to help change behavior.

Good luck with your goals. If, at times, you experience setbacks, regroup and remember that you can change, improve and grow. Believe in yourself—this is your most powerful tool and your most value asset. It's what will assure your success.

FOR THE EARLY BIRD

Living and Working
With the Punctually Challenged

This chapter is intended for those of you who live, work, and associate with the punctually challenged. Yours, as they say, is not an easy lot. You've had to deal with endless frustration, constant waiting, ruined dinner plans and creative excuses. You've probably been left cooling your heels outside movie theaters and drumming your fingers in restaurants more times than you can count. You've tried everything, from bribes and incentives to angry lectures and are bewildered as to why nothing seems to work.

As annoying as it may be for you, try to keep in mind that life can be pretty tough on the chronically late, too. They slink into meetings, sprint to airline departure gates and are frequently passed over for promotions. Their persistent tardiness is a source of embarrassment to them and a constant irritant to others.

What Makes the Tardy so Tardy?

There are a number of myths surrounding the motivations of the chronically late—attention seeking, not valuing the time of others and selfishness, among others. Certainly, there are late people who fall into those categories, and there does appear to be two camps among the tardy—those who care and those who don't. Most punctually challenged people, however, really do try to be on time.

Studies indicate that chronic lateness is most often a consistent, life-long habit, one that's surprisingly difficult to shake. Many late people share certain common characteristics, such as low self-control or high levels of anxiety—characteristics that influence their daily behavior and affect how sensitive they are to others.

There are seven types of late people and most folks fall into more than one category. In the pages to come, I'll briefly describe the different types and review ways to effectively deal with those punctually challenged people in your life.

The Seven Types of Late People

- The Rationalizer
- The Producer
- The Deadliner
- The Indulger
- The Absent-minded Professor
- The Rebel
- The Evader

As you read through the pages to come, remember, this chapter is not intended to excuse the sin of tardiness, but simply to help you understand and live with the punctually challenged.

Rationalization

Late people are often adept rationalizers. Of course, chronic lateness can be difficult to admit to, particularly when it's a habit that's often considered inconsiderate and irresponsible. Rationalization affects lateness in three ways: First, many tardy folks have difficulty admitting to the problem, insisting they're late only occasionally, and then only by a few minutes.

Second, because of the stigma chronic lateness carries, the punctually challenged have a tendency to under-rate the selfishness of the act. Defense mechanisms kick in, and they may even accuse you of being too uptight about time.

Third, those who do admit to problems with lateness often have difficulty owning up to their ability to control the situation, frequently blaming external factors, such as traffic jams, the kids or their busy schedules.

Compounding these rationalizations is the reluctance on the part of those waiting to chastise the late person. Because few people enjoy the unpleasant task of scolding, those left waiting often swallow their anger, smile graciously and accept any excuse offered. This allows tardy folks to blithely continue on course, minimizing the frustration they cause to others.

The Busy Syndrome

Another type of late person is the one who puts an emphasis on getting as much done in a day as possible. This individual, who I call the Producer, packs her days to the brim with a full-time job, errands, social events, volunteerism and a myriad of other activities. When she's swamped, she feels important and useful and her self-worth goes up a notch. However, instead of carefully planning and estimating how much she'll be able to accomplish in a specific period of time, she tries to do everything.

Many producers unwittingly engage in what I call "magical thinking," the ability to convince themselves that things will work out, even when all evidence is to the contrary. A typical scenario might play out like this: As Erin gets ready to go out for dinner, she looks at the clock and sees she only has ten minutes remaining to dry her hair, apply makeup, choose something to wear and get dressed. Intellectually, she knows that to do all this and still be on time is an impossible undertaking. Yet, she allows her mind to phase out reality and continues on her path, convincing herself that somehow everything will work out.

What causes this type of trick of the mind? More so than the timely, late folks have the ability to ignore reality, to see things as they want to see them. Of course, we all have blind spots that allow us to gloss over life. However, the punctually challenged seem to have a stronger than average tendency to do so, particularly when it comes to the clock.

Some late people also have an aversion to planning their days. Lacking a good daily plan, they consistently underestimate the amount of time their tasks will take. They dislike wasting time, so they attempt to time their arrivals to the minute. But naturally, timing activities this way rarely works out and lateness is often the result.

Deadlining

Another very common reason for chronic lateness is the tendency to seek out excitement and stimulation. This type of person, whom I call the "Deadliner," enjoys the rush of the last minute, the race to the finish line. Whether she's dashing around the house on her way out the door, or furiously jamming papers into her briefcase before a meeting, rushing makes her feel alive and focused. Deadliners typically fall into one or both of the following categories:

- Adrenaline junkies, for whom life is more enjoyable when there's excitement and urgency. Many punctually challenged folks enjoy the tension and stimulation induced by the last-minute frenzy and they have problems motivating themselves in the absence of a crisis. For some, just about the only way to get going is to wait until an urgent situation arises to push them along.

- Those for whom rushing is a way of relieving and distracting themselves from feelings of anxiety or boredom. Playing the game of "beat the clock" takes the focus off their feelings and gives them a sense of direction and purpose.

Some behavioral scientists believe that thrill-seeking has a psychologically addictive quality, comparable to compulsive eating, drinking or gambling. What's more, many believe that thrill-seeking, like other compulsive behaviors is, in part, a hereditary characteristic. One theory holds that a deficiency in the brain chemical serotonin is partially responsible for this tendency.

Discipline

Some studies suggest that late people as a group rank lower in self-control and have a lesser ability to make sacrifices than the timely. Many exercise less self-control not only in punctuality, but in other areas of life as well. My own research indicates that, overall, the punctually challenged do battle more bad habits than the punctual and more often have trouble resisting temptations. This doesn't mean that latecomers lack all self-control, but do tend to procrastinate more in general. These are people I refer to as "Indulgers."

Self-control is often a combination of hereditary physiological characteristics and environmental influences. If a child does not learn self-control early in life, he tends to have difficulty tolerating discomfort and making sacrifices later on. He learns to take the easy way out, the "gain with no pain."

The Rebel Syndrome

Another type of late person is the "Rebel," the person who feels compelled to break the little everyday rules that most people take in stride. Rebels often share three common characteristics:

- Unlike other categories of lateness, rebels often feel little remorse. "I get a sort of charge from keeping people waiting," says Larry, an accountant. "I kind of enjoy the control being late gives me."

- More men than women seem to populate this category. As one latecomer says, "It's a guy thing. You feel like you've got something over the next person if you can keep them waiting."

- This species of late people seem to have the ability to control their lateness more than other tardy types. Many report, for example, that they have no problem being on time to places or events that really matter to them, such as work, flights or interviews.

Tardiness by rebellion comes in three basic flavors: competing for power, resisting authority or attempting to feel special and unique. All three feel the need to regularly defy the rules, although they do so for different, but related reasons.

The first type of rebel is the power player, the person for whom showing up late is a way of feeling powerful. For this type of rebel, breaking the rules gives him a temporary boost and a feeling of control.

Ironically, the need to assert power usually stems from feelings of powerlessness in a person's life. The power player is often someone who has lower than average self-esteem and who thinks of lateness as a way of controlling the situation he is going into, a way of asserting his authority or superiority.

The second type of rebel is the authority resistor, the person who equates being accommodating with being weak. The routine compromises most of us see as the daily give and take of life, the authority resister sees as submission. This type of defiance is common among employees who resent some aspect of their jobs, be it the boss, salary, responsibilities or the policies of the company for whom they work. Employees who feel helpless to do anything constructive about their situation often opt for what is called "passive resistance," a way of outwardly appearing to comply, while inwardly resisting. Authority resistors are often the result of a childhood marked by overbearing or overcritical family influences.

More subtle than the power player and the authority resistor, yet just as tenaciously late, is the person who feels compelled to break society's rules out of a desire to stand out from the crowd. For the person who lacks a strong sense of self, bucking the rules is one way of bolstering self-esteem and feeling unique. It's a way of saying, "I'm different. I march to my own drummer." Actors, musicians and artists often populate this category.

The Absent-Minded Professor Syndrome

For other people, lateness results from a tendency to be easily distracted. Distractibility is thought to have a genetic basis, and can range from full-blown attention deficit disorder to simple absent-mindedness. It affects punctuality in two primary areas—the ability to stay focused on a course of action and the level of awareness one has to the needs and feelings of others.

People who are easily distracted have trouble keeping their attention focused on the task at hand without being pulled away to other activities. They have difficulty getting from point A to point B without being sidetracked by points C, D and E. On the way to the shower, the absent-minded professor passes the piano and sits down to play a few tunes. On the way out the door, he'll decide to water the lawn. Distractible folks also tend to have a tougher time with other attention matters—they lose track of time, misplace car keys and forget appointments.

Most distractible people don't intentionally cause aggravation and annoyance to those around them. In fact, they're puzzled when people say, "You just don't value my time," because valuing others' time is not something they're necessarily thinking about. Often they're just so preoccupied with their own thoughts or activities they don't stop to consider how their actions will affect others. Of course, we all tend to be most interested in what's going on in our own lives, but distractible people take this tendency a little further and chronic tardiness is one of the results.

Low Self-Esteem and High Anxiety

Studies indicate that late people as a group have lower levels of self-esteem and higher levels of anxiety than the timely. Because of these feelings, they may experience an overwhelming need to control their environments. They subconsciously feel that if they can make themselves and their surroundings perfect, they will feel less anxious. And it usually works...in the short run.

Lisa, for example, feels a sense of anxiety as she gets ready for a party. She's insecure about her personality, her looks and her ability to keep up a conversation. To alleviate her anxiety, Lisa tries to arrange the perfect situation for herself. She works out at the gym, shops for the perfect dress and fixes her hair just so. These activities do succeed in reducing her anxiety, but the need to perform them takes priority over getting out of the house on time. Even as she runs out of time, Lisa will continue with her planned routine.

People with low self-esteem sometimes have low expectations of themselves. They may put themselves in embarrassing or undignified situations where they're forced to apologize or make excuses—situations that people with high self-esteem try to avoid.

Low self-esteem and anxiety can be caused by a number of factors, among them childhood circumstances and genetic temperaments. While no one specifically inherits low self-esteem or anxiety, what is inherited seems to be a general personality type that predisposes a person to anxiety.

Temperament and Personal Choices

As far back as the 1930's, psychologists such as C. J. Jung found evidence that differences in behavior are related to the basic personalities we're born with. He suggested that while our families and environments influence the direction we go in, our basic dispositions remain relatively stable. Those dispositions, to a great degree, affect the things we like to do and the way in which we act.

Nowadays, most psychologists agree with Jung, believing that each individual is born with a distinct, unique temperament that has a profound effect on their behavior. Some personality types, such as sensitive ot anxious ones, may have more difficulty focusing on time and the task at hand.

Of course, the environment in which we're raised also has a tremendous influence on the way we develop into adulthood. While in some families, etiquette is an important part of the family culture, in others, a more lackadaisical sense of courtesy prevails. Children whose parents do not emphasize conformation to the "rules of society" will usually have a more flexible sense of how they should or should not behave.

The Choices We Make

While families and temperaments have a great impact on whether a person will turn out to be a considerate adult, an equal factor is the choices we make throughout our lives. Every choice a person makes affects their subsequent choices. For example, although she's pressed for time, Jane gives in to the temptation to have French toast instead of a bagel. The fact that she gave in to the French toast today makes her more likely to give in tomorrow. This is how the habit of lateness often starts—a onetime occurrence that, with each choice, takes a firmer hold.

TIPS FOR LIVING AND WORKING WITH THE CHRONICALLY LATE

How can you best deal with a late person without shouting, throwing things, storming out the door or firing them? It depends on two factors—the type of relationship you have and whether your late person wants to reform. Naturally, if you are married to a late person, your tactics will be different than those of an employer. The depth of your commitment to the punctually challenged will also affect your strategy and whether or not you're willing to stick it out while they're trying to change.

Following are some general principles that will help you to deal with late friends, family and colleagues. Later in this chapter, I'll provide specific advice on how to deal with late employees and managers as well as with dawdling children.

Don't take it personally. Try to understand that an individual's lateness is not a personal insult. It rarely has anything to do with not valuing your time or caring about your friendship. Most late people are not purposefully inconsiderate or rude. Remember that their lateness often impacts them just as negatively as it impacts you. They've spent their lives apologizing and feeling embarrassed. They've simply got a problem they need to get beyond.

Have a heart to heart talk. Discuss the problem openly and honestly. Let them know how much their lateness bothers you, but don't try to shame them into changing. Try to keep the conversation constructive and objective. In some instances, it might be appropriate to encourage late people to seek professional help, particularly if they seem to be in denial. Providing them a copy of this book is, of course, also a great place to start.

Be sure to initiate a talk before too much resentment builds. It's important to nip the problem in the bud and not wait until you're furious. If you delay talking about the problem until you're angry, you'll only succeed in hurting the late person and putting him on the defensive.

You may have already waited to confront your late person and are now at the point of throwing your hands in the air, jumping up and down and screaming. Try not to. As in any situation, the more calmly and amicably you can discuss things, the more success you'll have in helping the late person see the importance of change.

Agree on some parameters. Whether or not the late person acknowledges the problem, you can still set guidelines for the future. You might, for instance, agree to wait fifteen minutes before leaving without her. Or you may ask her to call if she's running behind. You might also agree to "ding" her for each occurrence. Agree that she'll buy coffee or dessert each time she's late or that she'll spring for the movie tickets.

Be ready to leave. It's important that the late person face the consequences of her actions. If you've agreed to wait fifteen minutes before leaving and that time has elapsed, leave. If you agreed she would buy desert, enforce the penalty. Be consistent in sticking to the guidelines you've set. Unfortunately, there are times when leaving can inconvenience you. For that reason, it may help to have some backup plans to assist in sticking to your guns.

If you do decide to wait, be sure to acknowledge that fact to the late person. Since most punctually challenged folks are adept at rationalizing, you'll only buy into that denial if you ignore the fact that she's late. You don't need to be unkind or harsh about it, but do calmly ask for an explanation, request that it not happen again, and move on. Don't hold a grudge or use the silent treatment. Simply let the late person know that you were inconvenienced and then let it go.

Provide encouragement. Be sure to compliment the late person for any progress, however slight. When she's ten minutes late instead of her usual thirty, give her a verbal pat on the back. You might say something along the lines of, "You're really making progress. I'm impressed."

Be careful, however, not to demoralize the late person by pointing out how inconsiderate she used to be. She's probably already painfully aware of how impolite she's been in the past and pointing it out will only insult her.

You may want to provide incentives for your late person, such as a nice dinner out, a weekend away or some small token of appreciation for the strides she's made. Showing her that you're on her side will help her feel optimistic and encouraged.

Remember that this is probably a lifelong habit. Be sure not to minimize the problem, as this rarely helps. Can you imagine telling a dieter to simply stop eating so much? Remember, every bad habit has its rewards, and late people typically receive some type of benefit, consciously or not, from being being late. Giving up that something, whether it's thrill-seeking, anxiety relief or some other payoff, can take time.

Have patience. Even after the late person understands why he is behaving the way he is, it will take some time to improve. Getting rid of an old habit is difficult, at best. Try to remember that much of what we do from day to day is automatic behavior. That's why bad habits are so hard to break. Even the most minor habits take time and determination to kick.

Keep in mind the many famous people who have gone public about conquering addictions to drugs or overeating. Even when they've made the announcement in front of millions of people, many have still had difficulty sticking with it.

Call ahead. If the late person is your doctor, hairdresser or other professional, try calling ahead to inquire if they're running behind schedule.

Try fudging a bit. If you plan to meet a friend for dinner at 8:00 p.m., tell him 7:30. Don't be too consistent with this method though. If you fib every time, the late person will eventually figure it out and adjust their schedule accordingly.

When meeting for a scheduled or reserved event—a movie, concert, or dinner—plan to meet for coffee a half hour before the event. This way, if the person you're meeting is late, you can always skip coffee without cutting into the planned event.

Accept the inevitable. Since your late person is probably not going to change overnight, accept that there will be times when you'll likely have to wait. Don't drive yourself crazy, instead, take a deep breath, relax and settle down. Try easing your frustration by preparing. Bring along a book, magazine or newspaper to keep occupied. It won't do you any good to sit and stew, so you may as well make the best of things.

Don't blow the issue of punctuality out of proportion. Sometimes lateness becomes such a sore point in a relationship that it takes on an importance beyond what it deserves. Take the case of Gerry and Natasha, who have been married for ten years. Natasha's constant tardiness upset Gerry so much that eventually he began to hit the roof when she kept him waiting only a minute or two. Gerry began to lose objectivity as to whether or not he was really inconvenienced.

"I became so focused on Natasha's lateness that I forgot about all her good qualities," explains Gerry. "I now regret some of my previous outbursts. If I could do it over, I'd have handled the situation differently."

MANAGING THE LATE EMPLOYEE

Employee lateness has long been ranked by business managers as a major employee-related problem in the United States. Tardiness costs U.S. companies an estimated $3 to $4 billion dollars each year in lost productivity. Perpetually tardy workers are not only expensive, but also have a negative influence on their co-workers. When an employee is allowed to repeatedly break the rules, his colleagues begin to build resentment and wonder why they're knocking themselves out to get in on time.

Late-arriving employees aren't the only problem employers face. Delayed meetings are a real problem in the corporate world, says Mark Ellwood, a consultant and trainer with Toronto-based Pace Productivity. "The fastest way to increase productivity in any organization is to start meetings on time," says Mr. Ellwood, whose company studies how employees spend their time. "There's a huge cost to people waiting around for meetings."

Of course, there are a myriad of motivations for chronic employee lateness, among them, job dissatisfaction, promotional or salary-related resentments or a lax company culture. If you suspect this to be the case, certainly investigate the problem. Sometimes, however, chronic lateness has nothing to do with the company, but is simply the problem of the individual employee.

Organizational Policy

The first step in eliminating chronic tardiness in an organization is to establish a corporate culture that encourages punctuality. Dan McMackin, a public relations manager with United Parcel Service, points to a corporate emphasis on punctuality as one of the factors that has led UPS to a leadership position in worldwide on-time deliveries. "Punctuality is a culturally entrenched notion at UPS," explains McMackin. "It's next to godliness, and it's nonnegotiable. Our culture embraces what Vince Lombardi, former coach of the Green Bay Packers, called 'Lombardi Time,' meaning, 'Be there fifteen minutes prior to start time.'"

UPS doesn't have a specific policy of reprimands or terminations for tardiness, but rather deals with the issue in a preventative way. They nip problems before they begin. As part of their new-hire orientation, employees are given a thorough understanding of corporate culture and of what is expected in terms of being on time. Managers are required to set good examples for employees, and all employees, regardless of rank, are rated in periodic performance reports that take into account punctuality.

"Because of the emphasis we place on punctuality, our employees don't think twice about showing up on time," explains McMackin. "They just do it."

Other managers find that an effective method of demonstrating the importance of a company's punctuality policy is to start meetings on time, locking the door when the meeting begins and discussing the most important issues early in the meeting.

To improve your employees' punctuality standards, start by taking a look at whether a punctuality policy has been established, communicated and consistently enforced. If your company doesn't currently have a policy, ask the human resources department to create one and to communicate it to all managers and employees. A typical punctuality policy is as follows:

- First occurrence: Verbal warning
- Three occurrences within one month: 1st written warning
- Three occurrences within one month following first written warning: 2nd written warning
- Three occurrences within one month following second warning: Termination

Individual Tardiness

In dealing with individual cases of chronic tardiness, the place to start is with a candid discussion. If you have a chronically late employee, start by explaining the tardiness policy and the importance of adhering to it. Some studies have shown a remarkable improvement in employee lateness when managers point out the ways in which their tardiness affects their coworkers. "They do get disturbed to realize that their coworkers see them as unreliable and untrustworthy," says Carolee Colter, principal of Community Consulting Group.

This is a good time to ask if there are particular reasons or extenuating circumstances why the employee can't comply with the policy. He may have justifiable logistical problems involving child or elder-care schedules. By bringing these issues into the open, you can discuss any options, such as flex or make-up time that might be available.

Frequently, however, the problem of lateness is not simply one of child care or scheduling, but rather one that involves personality issues such as those discussed earlier in this chapter. Chronically late people, as a rule, aren't usually aware of the underlying motives for their lateness, however. Even those who do understand their reasons may be hesitant to discuss their challenges with you. Furthermore, depending on your relationship with the employee, it may not be practical or appropriate to discuss personal issues. It is, however, appropriate to suggest reading material or seminars on procrastination, time management or chronic lateness.

Once you've eliminated logistical and scheduling conflicts, the next step in your discussion should be to set clear, measurable expectations for the future. It's not enough to ask the employee to improve their tardiness. Instead, set specific guidelines such as "Beginning June 1st, I'd like you to be at your desk at 8:00 a.m. every day." Be very specific in outlining your expectations and confirm the new guidelines in writing. Request that the employee sign written documentation and be sure to maintain copies for both yourself and human resources.

Be sure to clarify the consequences of being late in the future. You might state, "If you are more than ten minutes late three times within one month, you'll receive a written warning. If you are late more than nine times in three months, you will be dismissed." Let the employee know that you'll be monitoring and documenting each future occurrence.

The next part of your conversation should be to confirm the employee's understanding and encourage any questions or input. Then schedule a follow-up appointment to review their progress. This is critical. Setting a specific time for the next review will underscore the importance that you place on timeliness and remind the employee that this will be an on-going process.

Finally, don't hesitate to implement your punctuality policy when necessary. In many states, employers have the legal right to terminate or use a variety of disciplinary measures to deal with a chronically late employee. Companies are frequently allowed to dock the pay or vacation time of employees for each late occurrence.

Regardless of the penalty or incentive, managers should accurately document each instance of tardiness, every discussion with the employee and every action taken. These documents can be critical in the case of wrongful dismissal or discrimination suits.

There are times when you may want to consider positive incentives. Some research indicates that employees respond well to perks such as an extra day or two off or bonuses for perfect attendance. Several companies have found that providing parking spaces for employees with flawless punctuality records has paid off dramatically. Rick Vogeley, founder of a computer and video projection systems manufacturing plant in Newport News, Virginia, publishes a monthly list of employees with spotless attendance and gives out gift certificates and half-days off for the winners. "It sounds childish," Vogeley has said, "but it works."

Of course, it may go against your grain to reward behavior that is part of the normal course of employment. There are situations, however, where a few rewards go a long way toward making life easier for everyone.

Managers

What if your manager is the late person in the organization? The answer to that question is a tough one. Few employees relish the idea of chastising their managers. There are a few alternatives to biting your tongue, however.

First, start by getting your manager's attention by sending a free, anonymous lateness citation. Visit www.neverbelateagain.com, where you'll find your choice of two versions, a "kind, gentle" one and a "get tough" one.

Next, enlist the help of his or her assistant. Make it a habit to provide a copy of the meeting agenda and request the assistant's help in reminding the manager to arrive on time.

Finally, if you feel comfortable, broach the subject privately with the manager of human resources. Mention that you've noticed the company culture has become slack with regard to meeting start times and that productivity has become impacted. If your company lacks a human resource department, you may broach the subject directly with your manager, being careful not to point the finger at him or her personally.

Dealing with the Dawdling Child

It's 8:00 a.m., your child has to be to school at 8:30, and he still hasn't eaten his breakfast because he's busy looking for a missing backpack. You have two other children to dress and feed and your refrain of, "Come-on, let's go," is beginning to sound like an oversensitive car alarm blaring every few minutes—heard but largely ignored.

Sound familiar? Most parents have mornings like this. Even if you're usually a model of efficiency and organization, mornings can make you crazy. How can you prevent this kind of scenario without tearing your hair out or screaming yourself hoarse? The following tips usually work even in the most harried households:

Call a pow-wow with the kids. If they are old enough, sit down and talk with your little dawdlers about why they run behind. Do they have difficulty getting out of bed in the morning? Some research on circadian rhythms, for instance, indicates that the internal clocks that govern wakefulness and rest slow to a longer cycle in the teenage years. Children who in prior years bounded out of bed find the morning wake-up call a dreaded event in their teenage years. To compound things, many sleep researchers believe that teenagers have a physiological need for more sleep than do early adolescents, requiring a minimum of eight and a half hours each night.

For other children, hectic schedules may be the culprit. Just as the pace of our own lives seems to have increased dramatically in the past twenty years, so too have the lives of our children. If he's playing T-ball on Monday afternoons, swimming on Tuesdays, going to Cub Scout meetings on Wednesdays and attending piano practice on Thursdays, your child may just be tuckered out. If this sounds familiar, you may want to reevaluate your child's schedule. Talk about different alternatives that might help him or her change.

Work together to set goals and time schedules. Once you've taken the time to discuss the situation with your children, create a routine for each child with time frames in which they need to accomplish certain tasks. For instance, by 7:00 she must be out of bed, by 7:30 she must be dressed, by 7:50 she must be finished with breakfast.

Studies have shown that each child tends to have his or her own pace of doing things and trying to speed things up doesn't help much. For that reason, time frames for each child shouldn't necessarily be identical. For particularly pokey children, you'll want to have an earlier wake-up call and build in buffer time for tasks.

Create incentives for keeping to the schedule. Each day, keep track of who was on time and who wasn't and at the end of each week, reward children who have been consistently punctual. Don't hesitate to set individualized rewards for each child. As most parents know, what motivates one child doesn't always motivate another.

Develop a system of penalties. One mother I know docks her twelve-year-old's allowance by fifty cents for each day he's not dressed, fed and ready for school on time. Again, different penalties for different children are fine, as long as they are relatively equal. Be sure to stick to the penalties. Don't be swayed by imaginative excuses.

Don't do the broken-record routine. If you have to incessantly nag, you're defeating the purpose. The intent of these tips is to help get you out of the "Come on, get up" trap.

Prepare, prepare, prepare. Insist that children put in some prep time the night before. Homework should be gathered, backpacks should be packed, clothes should be decided upon and coats and hats should be placed by the door.

Get organized. Teach your children to have a place for everything. Keeping everyday items in the same place will help prevent that last minute search for books, backpacks and shoes. For additional ideas for getting organized, please review the tips in Cure Four.

Recognizing that parents aren't the only people who must deal with tardy tots, school administrators and teachers can also effectively fight tardiness by experimenting with their own punctuality policies. In schools throughout the country, administrators and teachers are turning around tardy students by following the example of Georgia's Norcross High and instituting a zero-tolerance policy. Students are locked out of class, given verbal warnings and finally suspended after repeated infractions.

Norcross isn't the only school that's cracked down on tardiness. Other schools throughout the country have experimented with incentives by offering rewards. Students with an A average and no more than three absences in one semester, for example, might skip a portion of their final exams. Some teachers have also found success with other positive incentives, such as giving out extra-credit assignments at the beginning of class when only prompt students are present.

Whether you're a friend, colleague, or employer of a late person, try to keep in mind that chronic lateness is not an easy habit to beat.

Even those who have a strong desire to change often have difficulty overcoming the tardiness trap. Although it may be tempting to say, "Just do it," try to restrain the impulse. Everyone—dieters, smokers and late people alike—performs better with encouragement and positive feedback. The tools in this book will help the late person. Your task will be to provide the support and patience necessary to achieve results.

APPENDIX A

Action Plan

1. Make an honest inventory of your past actions, and ask yourself if lateness has been a consistent—perhaps even lifelong—problem. Think of the times when the consequences were the most adverse. Relive the traffic tickets, reprimands, excuses, and missed opportunities.

2. Try to think about what your particular "benefit" for being late might be. Remember that we base our decisions, consciously or not, on the benefits versus the costs. Next, think of ways that being early will benefit you. Will it improve your reputation or your relationship with those around you? Will it increase your confidence or self-esteem?

3. Make timeliness a priority. Commit to being on time, all the time. Don't allow your punctuality to vary with the circumstance. Remember, you're in the process of breaking a long-ingrained habit and learning new habits takes repetition and reinforcement.

4. For the next three months, keep track on a daily basis of how often you are early, on-time or late. At the end of each

month, add up all the incidents in each category. This will help in monitoring your patterns and progress.

5. Relearn how to tell time. Write down the time you think it takes to accomplish everyday tasks. Over the next week, keep a notebook listing how long each activity actually took.

6. Overcome magical thinking by incorporating specific, concrete schedules into your daily life. Each day, sit down and plan your day, listing specific start and end times for each activity. Having a written schedule cements in your mind what you do and do not have time for.

7. Increase your willpower and tolerance for discomfort by practicing giving up something, just for a week. For example, if you normally drink two cups of coffee, drink one and a half for a week. Making little sacrifices will build your willpower and prepare you to resist the temptations that can make you late.

8. As a reminder not to procrastinate, post the following adage somewhere you'll see it every day: "It won't get any easier in five minutes." When you're tempted to put things off—such as getting out of bed in the morning—repeat this phrase to yourself.

9. Never plan to be exactly on time—always plan to be early. If you plan to be early, you'll probably make it just in time. Embrace the concept of "Lombardi Time" by always arriving fifteen minutes ahead of time.

10. When you are early, don't think of those extra minutes as wasted. Instead, begin to view waiting time as resting time, luxury time. Prepare for the wait. Bring a book, magazine or laptop to keep you busy, or just plan to sit and people watch.

11. When you feel the urge to squeeze in one more thing before leaving the house or office, use a signal such as a hand clap,

and ask yourself, "Is this really necessary to get where I'm going?"

12. Plan to get ready early enough to squeeze in something enjoyable, but nonessential just before you leave. By giving yourself that extra bit of leeway to practice the piano or to call a friend, you'll have a built-in buffer if getting ready takes longer than anticipated. You can always eliminate the activity if you run short of time.

13. Adopt the mantra, "Prepare, prepare, prepare." Practice it every day by gathering phones, keys, coats, laptops, umbrellas and other items you'll need to be out the door on time.

14. Practice starting and stopping. For example, when you're in the middle of an engrossing novel, but should be walking out the door, stop reading by telling yourself you can return to the book in five minutes if you really want to. When you're tempted to hit that snooze alarm a second time, tell yourself you can return to bed in five minutes. The law of inertia will typically take over. Remember, once in motion, you'll most likely remain in motion

15. Get out of the habit of saying, "If I hurry, I can…" When you're pressed for time, try to stop and remember what's important to you. Doing this several times a day will help you become more conscious of your decisions instead of being driven by your impulses.

16. Understand that cooperation is an everyday part of life. Practice "cooperation periods," when you comply with another person's expectations when normally you would resist. Instead of embracing the "me against them" philosophy, think of yourself as a team member, striving for what's best for everyone.

17. Begin to recognize when you're procrastinating because of

anxiety. The next time you're faced with a situation you're not sure you can handle, acknowledge your fear or hesitation. Practice positive self-talk by thinking of your feelings as those of excitement. Find one really positive thing to think about and focus all your attention on that one thing.

18. Add structure and organization to your life. Make regular time slots for activities, have specific places for everything and organize your house and office so that things are separate and easy to find.

19. Practice being more aware of others. Let go of any "me first" attitudes and try to understand how other people are thinking and feeling. Find ways to be as considerate and thoughtful as you can—remember birthdays, return phone calls in a timely manner and be generous with your time and compliments.

20. Learn how to meditate. Meditation will not only help you to relax, but it will also increase your awareness and willpower and your ability to focus on your goals.

APPENDIX B

Meditation Instructions

Stephan Bodian
Author of *Meditation for Dummies*

Though remarkably simple, meditation has the power to improve the quality of your life in extraordinary ways. Meditation can help to quiet your mind from life's daily stresses, relax your body, increase your focus and concentration and improve your health. Not surprisingly, today's hectic way of life has become commonplace for most of us. But more and more, people are turning to meditation for help in developing power and control over their lives and for gaining physical, mental and spiritual well-being. Here are some bare-bones instructions to help you get started.

1. Begin by sitting comfortably, with your back relatively straight but also relaxed. If possible, avoid leaning against anything, including the back of a chair. (For meditation, straight-backed chairs are generally better than cushy armchairs.) If you can't sit up straight, you can lie down or walk instead.

2. Take a few deep breaths, relaxing a little on each exhalation. Notice how your body feels as you sit (or lie or walk).

3. Now turn your awareness to the coming and going of your breath. Notice the rise and fall of your belly or chest as you breathe or the sensation of the air entering and leaving your nostrils. Let your attention focus softly but steadily on your breathing. When your mind wanders off (which it will do again and again), gently bring it back to the breath.

4. Continue to enjoy your breathing for five or ten minutes or longer. When you're done, stretch a little, then get up and go about your day.

Like any art, meditation has great subtlety and depth, and you can spend a lifetime cultivating and exploring the practice. But you can also gain enormous benefit from following this simple meditation for five or ten or fifteen minutes, day after day.

If you're new to meditation, you may have a list of questions you want to have answered before you're ready to get started. Well, here are answers to some of the queries I hear most frequently. For more in-depth responses, please pick up a copy of my book, *Meditation for Dummies*.

Question:

There seem to be dozens of different kinds of meditation available these days. Is there a single common thread that unites them all?

Answer:

Though the content may differ, most forms of meditation involve turning your attention inward, away from your usual preoccupations and activities, and focusing on a particular object, such as the breath, a mantra, a visualization, or a sound. In the process, you make the simple but significant shift from thinking and doing to just being. With repeated practice, your mind begins to settle down, your breathing slows, and you settle into a relaxed, peaceful, harmonious state. The thread that's common to all forms of meditation is the cultivation of awareness.

Question:

How can I tell the difference between one form of meditation and another? And how can I know which one would work best for me?

Answer:

Again, the primary difference lies in the content. If you have a particular spiritual or religious orientation, you may want to choose a method that accords with your values and beliefs. Otherwise, feel free to experiment with different approaches, practicing each for at least a few weeks to get the feel and the flavor before trying another. Trust your intuition or gut knowing on this one.

Some forms of meditation are designed to induce a particular state of mind or body. For example, healing meditations may help detoxify the body and stimulate the immune system, whereas meditations for opening the heart may guide you in extending love and compassion to others. Before you sign on for a course or a workshop or begin practicing a meditation, be sure you understand its intent. It's best to develop a regular foundation practice like following the breath, repeating a mantra, or focusing on a sound or other sensory object, to which you can add specialized meditations as you feel inclined.

Question:

I understand that meditation builds concentration and might help me increase my focus at work and in my daily life. Can you explain how it might do that?

Answer:

When you meditate, you train your mind to stay focused on a particular object—and when it wanders off, you gently bring it back. With repeated practice, your mind develops the power or capacity to stay focused for extended periods of time. Just as when you lift weights regularly, your muscles get stronger and stronger, so when you meditate regularly, your mental muscles get stronger, too.

Question:

I'm drawn to meditation because I just can't get a grip on my agitated mind. I'm either agonizing over what happened yesterday or worrying about what might happen tomorrow. How can meditation help me work with my mind?

Answer:

Here again, the practice of bringing your mind back again and again—to your breath, your body, a mantra or a sound—can have a powerful impact on the rest of your life.

Develop this mental muscle, and when your mind starts worrying or obsessing, you can gently lead it away from its painful or frightening preoccupations and back to the present moment. As a result, instead of spinning out of balance when difficulties arise, you stay centered, grounded, and balanced.

Question:

Is meditation just something you do on a cushion or chair every now and then, or can you extend your meditation into other areas of your life, like driving or working or taking care of the kids?

Answer:

Well, the cushion or chair part is extremely important, and you're better off doing it daily, rather than every now and then. Pretty soon you'll start noticing that you're more relaxed, centered, and peaceful at other times of the day as well.

But you can also consciously extend your meditation to other activities by being mindful of what you're doing, rather than spacing out or daydreaming. You can drive your car or talk on the phone or work at your computer with the same careful attention you bring to your meditation.

Question:

I'm afraid that meditation will turn me into a zombie or a space cadet. I need to feel a certain level of anxiety or tension in order to function. How can I be sure that I won't lose my drive?

Answer:

Instead of turning you into a zombie or space cadet, meditation will do just the opposite—it will bring you down out of the clouds and into the present moment, where your life is actually taking place. (Remember the John Lennon line, "Life is what's happening while you're busy making other plans"?) Though your level of anxiety and tension may drop (hallelujah!), you won't sacrifice your drive or energy. Quite the contrary: People who meditate regularly report that they get their work done more effectively and get more enjoyment from life.

Question:

I'm a real body-oriented person, and meditation seems too cerebral for me. Can you meditate with your body as well as your mind?

Answer:

Though you're using the mental muscle known as attention, you're actually bringing the body, breath, and mind into harmony when you meditate. Yes, certain meditations are more body-oriented—for example, counting or following your breath, tracking your sensations, or focusing on a particular part of the body.

Question:

These days everyone seems to be rushing from one appointment or activity to the next. How can I find the time in my busy life to sit quietly for ten or fifteen minutes?

Answer:

How can you afford not to? Although external circumstances may make constant demands on your time and attention, stress is actually an internal experience caused by how you interpret events. Through regular meditation, you can learn to slow your mind down and create an inner spaciousness so you don't feel so pressured in your mind and heart, where it really counts. As for finding the time, most people can carve out a brief oasis in the morning or evening. Once you begin enjoying your meditation, you'll feel motivated to do it regularly and perhaps even extend the length of time from ten or fifteen minutes to twenty or thirty.

Question:

I've tried to meditate, but I just end up falling asleep or spacing out. I must be doing something wrong. What can I do to remedy the situation?

Answer:

It's actually quite common to fall asleep or space out. If you're physically tired, perhaps you need to get more sleep or take a nap. Otherwise, you can make an effort to increase your mental focus, open your eyes rather than close them, or even get up and walk around or splash some cold water on your face before resuming your meditation.

Question:

What can I do about the restlessness or discomfort I feel when I meditate?

Answer:

Another common "obstacle" in meditation, restlessness can take many forms. If your mind is extremely agitated, you might want to increase your focus, as I mentioned earlier. Or do some deep body relaxation before you meditate (or in place of your meditation) to help calm you down. If you're physically uncomfortable, try shifting your position, though it's best to stay as still as you can while you meditate. When your concentration gets stronger, you can just observe your restlessness without allowing it to disturb your meditation.

Question:

How can I tell if I'm meditating the right way? How do I know if my meditation is working?

Answer:

The great thing about meditation is that it doesn't "work." Instead, it provides an unprecedented opportunity to set aside the attitude of work and just be, without any expectations or agendas. Wheww, what a relief! If you find yourself wondering whether you're doing it right, just notice those thoughts and gently return to the object of your meditation, such as your breath or a mantra. The operative word here is "gently."

Question:

I generally associate meditation with Buddhists or Hindus in their loin cloths or robes. What about those of us who consider ourselves Christian or Jewish or Muslim? Do we have to give up our religion in order to meditate?

Answer:

Absolutely not. In fact, you can use meditation to deepen your understanding and experience of any religious tradition. If the great religions are rivers, then meditation is a current that runs through them all. In particular, Christianity and Judaism have recently rediscovered their own meditative practices in response to the influx of Eastern teachers and teachings, and they have also incorporated techniques drawn from Buddhism, Hinduism, Sufism, and yoga. For more info, check out *Meditation For Dummies*.

Stephan Bodian is the author of *Meditation for Dummies*, a comprehensive, user-friendly guide to the practice of meditation. He is also an ordained Zen Buddhist priest, former editor-in-chief of the magazine, *Yoga Journal,* and a nationally recognized expert on meditation and spirituality. Stephan graduated Phi Beta Kappa from Columbia University and did graduate work at Stanford. As a psychotherapist, phone-based personal and executive coach, and spiritual mentor, he is available by phone to clients worldwide. For more information or to contact him, please visit his web site at www.stephanbodian.com.

Bibliography

Amen, Daniel, M.D. *Don't Shoot Yourself in the Foot.* New York: Warner Books, 1992.

—*Change Your Brain, Change Your Life*, New York: Times Books, 2002.

Backus, William. *Finding the Freedom of Self-control.* Beghany House Publishers, 1987.

Baumeister, Roy F., Todd F. Heatherton, and Dianne M. Tice. Losing Control: *How and Why People Fail at Self-regulation.* Burlington, Mass: Academic Press, 1994.

Bliss, Edwin C. *Doing It Now: How to Cure Procrastination and Achieve Your Goals in 12 Easy Steps.* New York: Simon & Schuster, 1986.

Bourne, Edmund J., PhD. *The Anxiety & Phobia Workbook.* Oakland, Calif.: New Harbinger Pub., 1995.

Branden, Nathaniel, Ph.D. *The Power of Self-Esteem.* Deerfield Beach, Fla.: Health Communications, Inc., 1992.

Burka, Jane B., Ph.D. and Lenora M. Yuen, Ph.D. *Procrastination: Why You Do It and What to Do About It.* Reading, MA: Addison Wesley Publishing, 1983.

Carlson, Richard, Ph.D. *Don't Sweat the Small Stuff.* New York: Hyperion, 1997.

Cook, Marshall J. *Slow Down and Get More Done.* Cincinatti, Ohio: Betterway Books, 1993.

Davidson, Jeff. *The Complete Idiot's Guide to Managing Stress.* New York: Alpha Books, 1997.

Douglass, Merrill E. and Douglass, Donna N. *Manage Your*

Time, Your Work, Yourself. New York: AMACOM, 1993.

Eisenberg, Ronni with ate Kelly. *Organize Yourself!* New York: MacMillan, 1997.

Gasser, William, M.D. *Take Effective Control of Your Life.* New York: Harper & Row, 1984.

Goldfriend, Marvin. *Behavior Change Through Self-Control.* Austin, Texas: Rinehart, Holt and Winston.1973.

Goleman, Daniel. *Emotional Intelligence.* New York: Bantam Books, 1995.

Hallowell, Edward M., M.D., and John J. Ratey, M.D. *Answers to Distraction.* New York: Bantom Books, 1994.

—*Driven to Distraction.* New York: Touchstone Book, Simon & Schuster, 1994.

Hamstra, Bruce, Ed.D. *Why Good People Do Bad Things.* Secaucus, N.J.: Carol Publishing Group, 1996.

Horn, Sam. *Concrete Confidence.* New York: St. Martin's Press, 1997.

Jeffers, Susan, Ph.D. *Feel the Fear and Do It Anyway.* New York: Fawcett Columbine, 1987.

Lehmkuhl, Dorothy and Dolores Cotter Lamping, CSW. *Organizing for the Creative Person.* New York: Crown Trade Paperbacks, 1993.

Logue, A. W. *Self-Control.* Paramus, N.J.: Prentic Hall, 1995.

Mahoney, Michael J. and Carl E. Thoressen. *Self-Control: Power to the Person.* Belmont, Calif: Wadsworth Pub., 1974.

McGinnis, Alan Loy. *The Balanced Life: Achieving Success in Work and Love.* Minneapolis: Augsburg Fortress, 1997.

McGraw, Nanci. *Organized for Success.* Mission, Kansas: Skillpath Publications, 1995.

Mishove, Jeffrey, Ph.D. with Shinzen Young. *Thinking Allowed: Overcoming Compulsive Behavior.* Video.

"Paucity of Punctuality Costs Americans Over $3 Billion a Year." Business Wire. 1998.

Rifenbary, Jay with Mike and Marjie Markowski. *No Excuse!* Hummelstown, Penn. Markowski International Publishers, 1996.

Sapadin, Linda, Ph.D. with Jack Maguire. *It's About Time: The 6 Styles of Procrastination and How to Overcome Them.* New York: Viking Press, 1996.

Seligman, Martin P., Ph.D. *What You Can Change and What You Can't.* New York: Alfred A. Knopf, 1994.

Simon, Sidney B., Ed.D. *Getting Unstuck: Breaking Through Your Barriers to Change.* New York: Warner Books, 1988.

Smith, Hyrum W., *The 10 Natural Laws of Successful Time and Life Management.* New York: Warner Books, 1994.

Snead, G. Lynne and Joyce Wycoff. *To Do, Doing, Done.* NewYork: Fireside Book, Simon and Schuster, 1997.

Sudderth, David B., M.D. and Kandel, Joseph, M.D. *ADD: The Complete Handbook.* Rocklin, Calif.: Prima Publishing, 1997.

Thomas, Alexander, M.D. and Stella Chess, M.D. *Temperament and Development.* New York: Brunner/Mazel, Publishers, 1977.

Walker, Michael B., *The Psychology of Gambling.* Pergamon Press, 1992.

Whiteman, Thomas A., Ph.D. and Michele Novotoni, Ph.D. *Adult ADD.* Colorado Springs, Colorado: Pinon Press, 1995.

Wishnie, Howard, M.D. *The Impulsive Personality.* New York: Plenum Press, 1977.

Footnotes

[1]From data provided by the United States Bureau of Census, the United States Department of Commerce, and Westclox Incorporated.

Index

Media and Ordering Information

Author Interviews: *Never Be Late Again* has been featured on *The Today Show, Good Morning America, NBC News, NPR Radio, BBC Radio, The New York Times, The London Times* and hundreds of other national and international media. To arrange an interview with Diana DeLonzor, please contact Kit Carson at Post Madison Publishing at info@postmadisonpublishing.com.

Book Orders: To order additional or bulk copies of *Never Be Late Again,* please contact info@postmadisonpublishing.com or visit our website, www.neverbelateagain.com.

Lateness Citations: To order a free anonymous lateness citation for the punctually challenged person in your life, please visit www.neverbelateagain.com.

Post Madison Publishing

www.postmadisonpublishing.com

Please like us on Facebook at:

Facebook.com/Never Be Late Again